ART AND HISTORY
SAN FRANCISCO

BONECHI
SNC

Distribution by
smith NOVELTY COMPANY
460 Ninth Street
San Francisco, CA 94103
U.S.A.
Phone: 415 - 861-4900
Fax: 415 - 861-5683

e-mail address: snco@smithnovelty.com
web site: www.smithnovelty.com
Toll Free 1-888-861-SNCO (7626)

CONTENTS

© Copyright by Casa Editrice Bonechi - Florence - Italy
Tel. +39 055576841 - Fax +39 0555000766 / E-mail: bonechi@bonechi.it - Internet: www.bonechi.it; www.bonechi.com

Publication created by Casa Editrice Bonechi. Publication manager: Monica Bonechi.
Photographic research by the Editorial Staff of the Casa Editrice Bonechi. Editing: Anna Baldini, Giovannella Masini. Graphic design, layout and cover: Manuela Ranfagni.
Drawings pages 4-5,18-19, 54-59 by Stefano Benini. Drawings pages 12-13 by Sauro Giampaia. Map by Daniela Mariani. Text by Robert Fitzgerald and Maria Elena Velardi.
Pages 140-143: text by Richard Dunbar. Pages 12, 13: text by Filippo Bonechi translated by Paula Boomsliter.
The Mission District Murals: page 106: "Keep Our Ancient Roots Alive" © 1995 by Susan Kelk Cervantes. On Cleveland Elementary School at Persia and Athens Streets;
page 107 "Family Life & The Spirit of Mankind" © 1977 by Susan Kelk Cervantes & Judith Knepher Jamerson. On Flynn Elementary School, at Harrison & Precita Streets;
pages 1 (center photo), 108/109: "Carnaval" © 1996 by Josh Sarantitis, Emmanuel Montoya, and Precita Eyes Muralists. At Harrison and 19th Street;
page 110: "Silent Language of the Soul/ El Lenguaje Mudo del Alma" © 1990 by Susan Kelk Cervantes & Juana Alicia. On Cesar Chavez Elementary School, on Shotwell
between 22nd & 23rd Streets

PHOTOGRAPHY ACKNOWLEDGMENTS
Photographs from the archives of Casa Editrice Bonechi taken by Andrea Pistolesi.
David M. Allen: *page 91 bottom right.* Richard Brackett: *pages 10, 11.* Ken Glaser: *17 bottom, 24-25, 26, 27 bottom, 29 center and bottom, 32 top and center right, 35 center
and bottom, 36-37, 40 bottom, 42, 43 right, 47, 51, 56/59, 63 bottom, 76, 85, 86, 90, 91 top, 93, 94 bottom, 95, 98 top, 100, 101, 102 bottom left, 103, 104, 106/110
111 center left, 113 bottom, 116, 118 center and bottom, 121/123, 124 top, 126, 128, 129, 130 top left, 131, 132, 133 top and center, 134 top, 136 top and center, 147, 148
bottom left,152 top, 153 center, 155 top and bottom, 158 bottom, 159 bottom.* Matt Kastner: *page 158 top.* Andrew McKinney: *pages 3, 38-39, 48-49, 60-61, 69, 102 bottom
right, 117, 125 top, 133 bottom, 136 bottom, 138 bottom, 146 top, 149 top, 156-157.* George Olson: *page 146 center right.*
Photographs Courtesy of Asteron Production: *page 141 bottom right;* Cathedral Conference Center Saint Mary's Cathedral/*Property of Sisters of the Holy Family, 656-2263*
(ph. John Wright): page 66 top; © The Exploratorium San Francisco: *page 83;* Fine Arts Museums of San Francisco (FAMSF): *pages 77 top (ph. Owen Mc Goldrick) and
bottom, 78, 79, 80, 81;* Golden Gate National Recreation Area, Don Denevi Photographic Collection: *pages 141 center and bottom left, 143;* Golden Gate National Recreation
Area, Photographic Collection: *151 bottom (ph. Willliam C. Billington).* Hotel Triton, Kimpton Group: *page119 top right and center;* Marilyn Blaisdell Collection: *pages 8, 9,
16, 17 top, 33, 46, 97 bottom, 148 center left, 149 bottom, 150 bottom, 151 top, 159 top;* Museum of Craft and Folk Art: *page 127, top photos;* San Francisco African American
Historical and Cultural Society: *page 127, bottom photos (center bottom: ph. David Johnson);* San Francisco Maritime National Historical Park, Photographic Collection: *pages
6-7, 151 center;* SF MOMA: *page 68 left: top, center, bottom (ph. Richard Barnes); pages 72, 73 (center left: © Charly Herscovici c/o A.R.S., New York), 74, 75 (top right and
center left: ph. Ben Blackwell);* Wells Fargo Bank: *pages 5, 84.*
The publisher would like to thank Ken Glaser for his invaluable assistance
The publisher apologizes for any unintentional omissions. We would be pleased to include any appropriate acknowledgments of which we are informed in subsequent editions of this publication.

* * *

INTRODUCTION

America's favorite city, San Francisco sits perched above one of the world's most beautiful junctures of land and sea.

Surrounded on three sides by water, San Francisco is foremost a city of exquisite views. First-time visitors and age-old residents alike are amazed every day by the awesome sight of the sun rising over San Francisco Bay and the twilight fog enveloping the Golden Gate Bridge and the surrounding hills. Around each corner and at the crest of every hill, San Francisco's natural beauty sets it apart from all of the other great cities of the world.

For all of its geographical splendor, however, what makes San Francisco unique is the people who live there. Throughout the city's history, San Francisco has been defined by the distinctive and unusual personalities of those who venture to settle there.

San Francisco sits at the edge of the Western World, the furthest boundary of the proverbial final frontier. This mythical location, of course, only adds to the city's romance and legend. From its origins as a Gold Rush outpost, San Francisco has captured the imagination of the world's pioneers and frontiersmen. Generation after generation, San Francisco has attracted those who wish to make that metaphorical journey Westward in search of new frontiers. San Francisco has been home to some of history's most colorful personalities and frontiersmen. The early gold surveyors, pioneers and sailors gave way to waves of merchants, barons and boomtown entrepreneurs, immigrants, poets, writers, artists, bankers, prostitutes, bums and rapscallions - all before the turn of the century.

In modern times, San Francisco has stood at the edge of cultural frontiers and has often been called the New Bohemia. Progressive idealism has been San Francisco's trademark. In the 1950s, the Beat Generation thrived in San Francisco, transforming North Beach's cafes, wine bars and jazz clubs into the breeding ground of a revolutionary new form of artistic self-expression.

Less than a decade later, Flower Power descended on San Francisco, again transforming the city and symbolizing the ideals of an entire generation of Americans. In the 1970s and '80s, socio-political movements like free speech, gay rights, holistic health and the environment kept the city at the forefront of progressive thought and action.

What is amazing about San Francisco is its ability to reinvent itself over and over again. Less than 150 years ago, San Francisco was a backwater city of tents and mud. Today the city is home to a new breed of pioneer and frontiersman, the technological wizards of Silicon Valley who rule the cyber universe. San Francisco is a major international city. After New York, it is the second most densely populated city in the U.S. Yet, San Francisco's inherent natural beauty and its powerful human character belie that fact. Unlike so many other modern metropolises - hollow canyons of glass, steel and brick - San Francisco has both heart and soul.

Aerial view of Financial District.

THE BEGINNINGS

T he San Francisco bay area was originally inhabited by nomad populations of the Ohlone tribe of the Miwok linguistic group. The first European settlement was instead founded in 1776: on June 27th of that year, Juan Bautista de Anza landed on the shores of the bay and officially took possession of the area in the name of the Spanish crown. The Spanish

San Francisco's inhabitants, from the native Ohlones to the prospectors and permanent settlers.

explorer immediately began building the city's first edifice: the fort known as the Presidio that still dominates the Golden Gate.
A few months later, a Franciscan monk built the first mission. It was dedicated to his patron saint, from whom the city took its name.
Quite soon the profitable trade in pelts made San Francisco a compulsory stop for the merchant ships plying the western coast of the North American continent.
In 1821, Mexico declared its independence from Spain, and in 1847

California became a territory of the United States. After gold was discovered at Sutter's mill in 1848 and the ensuing California Gold Rush brought thousands of immigrants to San Francisco, the city's extraordinary population growth and economic expansion began in earnest.

THE GOLD RUSH

Wells Fargo Bank History Museum: Gold Rush balance scales.

Word that gold nuggets had been found in the American River inland of San Francisco began to spread in early 1848. It wasn't long before the city was invaded by thousands of people determined to get rich quick: in fact, in just a few months the population of San Francisco jumped from 800 to 25,000! The following year, when the majority of the gold seekers arrived and set up housekeeping in a tent village on the slopes of the hill, the local merchants made small fortunes selling equipment and supplies at exorbitant prices. The arrival of the Forty-Niners transformed San Francisco into one of the world's most cosmopolitan cities: England, Ireland, Poland, Mexico, Chile, and China were only a few of the nations represented in the tide of foreign immigrants and Americans from all over the United States. When the California Gold Rush ended in 1852, only a few of the 150,000 prospectors who had come through the city's port in those four hectic years had made the fortune they dreamed, but many nevertheless decided to settle in and around San Francisco and make their lives there.

Jack London (1876-1916)

San Francisco was the birthplace of Jack London, one of the most popular American writers of the 20th century and certainly the author who best narrated the pioneer spirit of the city and its inhabitants. After completing his secondary studies in the classics, London went prospecting in Alaska in 1897/98 during the great Klondike Gold Rush. On his return he published a collection of short stories that drew heavily on his experiences. The most famous of all his writings is of course the novel *The Call of the Wild* (1903).

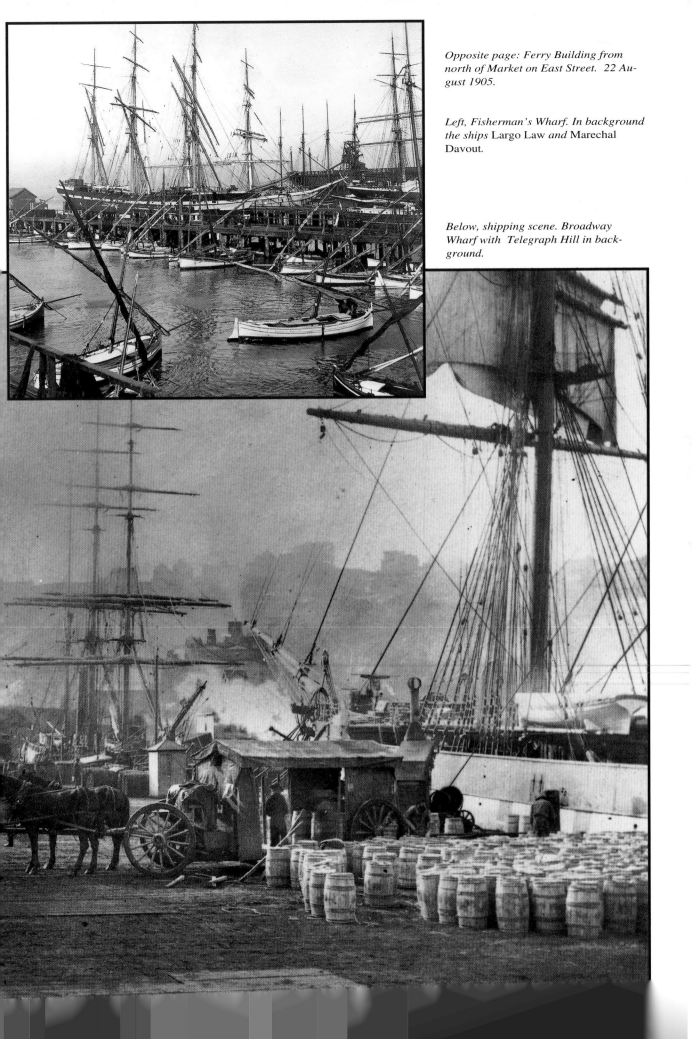

Opposite page: Ferry Building from north of Market on East Street. 22 August 1905.

Left, Fisherman's Wharf. In background the ships Largo Law *and* Marechal Davout.

Below, shipping scene. Broadway Wharf with Telegraph Hill in background.

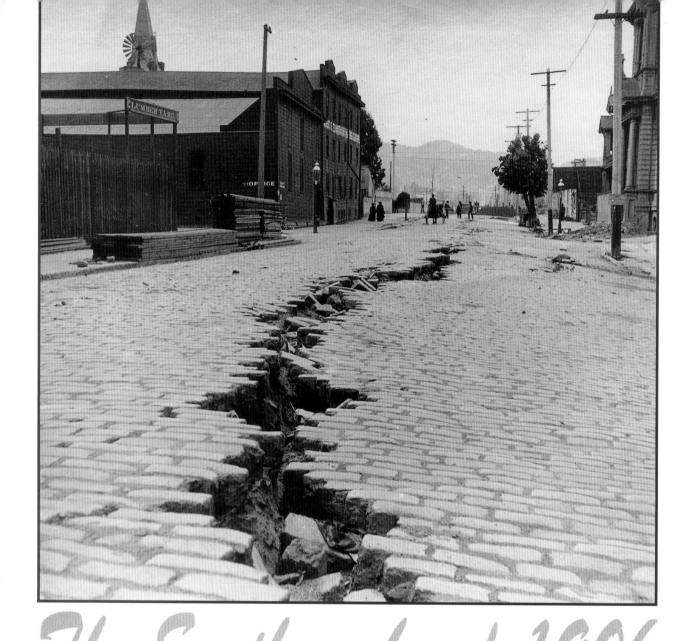

THE EARTHQUAKE OF 1906

It was a little after 5:00 a.m. on the morning of 18 April 1906 when the population of San Francisco was awakened by one of the strongest earthquakes of the modern era. The intensity and the duration varied from place to place, but in just a few instants the streets of the city filled with frightened, disoriented citizens. A major aftershock shook the city again at 8:14, bringing down even more buildings. And so began the fire that raced through the city for three days, almost completely destroying the center and a goodly part of the residential neighborhoods. The area around the San Andreas fault was the hardest hit, but enormous damage was also wreaked between 17th Street and 19th Street, Dolores Street and Potrero Avenue, and between Mission, Seventh, Harrison, and Fourth Streets.
The first buildings to fall were the Masons' Temple, City Hall, the Mechanics Pavilion, the Winchester Hotel, the Hearst Building, Saint Mary's Hospital, and the Central Fire Alarm Station. At 2:30 p.m., the army decided to use dynamite to stop the spread of the fire, which was threatening the Mint on Fifth and Mission. But the flames continued spreading in many other parts of the city. That evening, to make things worse, a pyromaniac fired Delmonico's restaurant and the Alcazar theater. The St Francis Hotel on Union Square was one of the first buildings to catch fire on 19 April. Late in the day, Colonel Charles. Morris of the Artillery Corps ordered the mansions along Van Ness Avenue razed in the hope of creating a firebreak. Despite these measures, the fire continued to spread in other directions; on the morning of 20 April, the more than 20,000 homeless were evacuated on the USS Chicago. On the 21st, the fire destroyed the Mission District before it was stopped at 20th Street and Dolores by 3,000 volunteer firemen. It was finally brought under control the next day, and by the 23rd the flames had been extinguished all over the city. The toll in lives and property was astounding: more than 3,000 dead and 500 million 1906 dollars in property damage.

1906

The earthquake and resulting fire deeply wounded San Francisco, which since the late 19th century had been the US's major west coast city and second only to New York in size and wealth. But the calamity of 1906 was not the first time the city had been tried by fire, and reconstruction began immediately. Less than ten years later, San Francisco was once again the splendid city of old and ready to host the 1915 Panama Pacific International Exposition held to celebrate the opening of the Panama Canal—and the exceptional rebirth of this just as exceptionally resourceful city.

The 1906 Earthquake. Right, the ruins of the Clock Tower. Bottom of page, a view of the damage wreaked by the quake and fire in the San Francisco Hills.
Opposite, a crack down the center of a San Francisco street.

Jack London on the Earthquake of 1906

"Not in history has a modern imperial city been so completely destroyed. San Francisco is gone. Nothing remains of it but memories and a fringe of dwelling-houses on its outskirts. Its industrial section is wiped out. Its business section is wiped out. Its social and residential section is wiped out." Jack London (first published in *Collier's*, 5 May 1906).

25

THE EARTHQUAKE OF 1989

1989 Earthquake. SF-Oakland Bay Bridge.

The worst earthquake to rock San Francisco after the catastrophe of 1906 was the Loma Prieta (World Series) quake, which hit at about 5:00 p.m. on 17 October 1989. Although the city was not destroyed as it was at the beginning of the century, there was no lack of apocalyptic scenes on this occasion either. Damages amounted to almost 3 billion dollars; the city was blacked out for two days. Twenty-seven fires broke out in various urban areas and, like in 1906, the fire-fighters were aided by private citizens who manned bucket brigades in those areas where the water mains were broken. The 7.1 Richter magnitude quake was so strong as to cause the collapse of a part of the San Francisco - Oakland Bay Bridge and to sink an entire residential complex in the Marina neighborhood into an artificial lagoon. The 1989 earthquake left more than 12,000 homeless and caused 6 deaths in San Francisco and a total of 62 in California as a whole.

Below and opposite, damaged buildings in the Marina District.

1989

A "GEOWORD" ABOUT SAN FRANCISCO

One of the many reasons San Francisco is one of the world's most famous cities is its geological situation. The city is in fact crossed by the infamous San Andreas Fault, which, on its nearly 1000 kilometer course, runs from Imperial Valley to Point Andrea. The fault is the major geological structure in all California—and it has even become a sort of a dark symbol of the state. It, and the enormous fault system of which it is part, give California its less-than-enviable place on the hit parade of the world's most seismically unstable areas, where telluric movements of intensities from mild to catastrophic are the order of the day. San Francisco suffers small earthquakes almost every day, but the people of the area are used to living with them—and actually live quite well, thanks to constant improvement in the field of anti-seismic construction technology. But despite all this, the peace of mind of many of California's residents is disturbed by thoughts of the "Big One," an earthquake of devastating proportions that they expect will someday detach California from the North American continent in one fell swoop. San Francisco's history so far records two big earthquakes: the catastrophic 1906 quake, magnitude 8 on the Richter scale, that with the consequent fire left in its wake 3000 dead and hundreds of millions of dollars in damage,

and the 7.1 Richter magnitude quake of October 1989, when the damages were much more limited in scope—above all in terms of lives lost.

In order to better understand the nature of the San Andreas Fault we must first look at the "Tectonic Plate Theory" that today explains the movements of the earth's crust and that has gained much and has also been widely confirmed by observation of the morphological evolution of the California area. This theory tells us that the earth's crust is subdivided into a series of gigantic plates (see Figure 1) in perennial movement—and therefore in reciprocal and constant collision and transformation. The area where the plates collide are those subject to earthquakes, volcanic phenomena, and orogenesis (formation of mountains).

The San Andreas Fault is the most spectacular surface manifestation of the stresses between the Pacific Plate and the North American Plate. These collisions result in reciprocal horizontal displacements (see Figure 2) of the two plates; due to the type of movement along it, San Andreas Fault is defined as a "right lateral strike-slip" fault. The average speed of the northward movement of that part of California west of the fault has been measured since 1800 at about 6 cm per year.

1 *Fig. 1 (World)*
As we can see, the Earth's crust is divided into a certain number of enormous plates. Gigantic forces generated by complex physical-chemical processes deep inside our planet subject the plates to constant motion that makes them hit, overlap and separate from each other. This motion continuously changes their shapes and respective positions. It is in the contact area between plates, shown by the red lines, that earthquakes occur, volcanoes are formed and mountains develop, demonstrating the earth's geological vitality. The continents, as we see in the illustration, are merely more or less extensive parts of the plates.

Eurasian

North American

Eurasian

Caribbean

Arabian

Pacific

Cocos

South American

Indo-Australian

Nazca

African

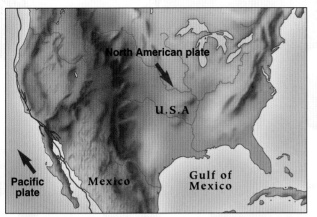

Fig. 2 (North America)
The illustration shows that the entire North American continent is part of the North American plate except for a small strip of land: the California coast that is part of the Pacific plate.
In the area between the two plates, known as the plate margin, a complex system of cracks have formed. In technical terms these cracks are known as faults. One of the biggest and longest of these is the famous San Andreas Fault that runs along nearly the entire California coast. Here, the two plates shift horizontally alongside of each other: the Pacific plate moves North-Northwest and the North American plate shifts South-Southeast. This horizontal movement is known as transforms and the faults where they occur are called transform faults.

Fig. 3 (San Francisco)
As we zoom in closer, we see that in addition to the San Andreas Fault San Francisco sits on other major ones including the Calaveras and Hayward faults, which together with the San Andreas represent the main tectonic structures. Therefore, it is not difficult to see why this is one of the most seismic areas on the entire planet.

Golden Gate Bridge

San Francisco's most powerful icon, the Golden Gate Bridge is arguably the most beautiful bridge in the world. Spanning a beautiful land and seascape bound by the hills of Marin on one side and the Presidio on the other, the bridge is also remarkable for its graceful lines, unique color, Moderne accents and even the sublime, evocative currents of fog that often obscure it.

Joseph B. Strauss was chief engineer of the project and Clifford Paine supervised construction, which was begun in 1933 and finished four years later. The total cost of the project was $33 million; that sum was finally paid off by bridge tolls in 1971. Before construction began, there were many protests against the project, which would greatly alter the natural landscape at the mouth of the bay. When the 4,200-foot span was completed, however, there were few nay-sayers.

Until New York's Verrazzano Bridge was built in 1959, the Golden Gate was the longest continuous bridge span in the world. The roadway hovers 276 feet above the water, while the art-deco towers rise yet another 470 feet. The suspension cables that keep the bridge aloft are over thirty-six inches wide. Midway across, the bridge was built to sway up to twenty-seven feet in high winds or earthquakes, which certainly doesn't alleviate pedestrian vertigo. Walkways were included in the design of the bridge, offering spectacular views; the one-way hike is about 1.2 miles. The Golden Gate Bridge is the most photographed man-made structure in the world.

THE HISTORY

O ne of the world's most famous bridges takes its name from the strait it spans at the entrance to San Francisco Bay from the Pacific Ocean. In 1846, Captain John C. Fremont of the Engineer Corps of the US Army dubbed the strait "Chrysopylae" (Greek for "Golden Gate," in fact) because it reminded him of the port of Istanbul, called "Chrysoceras" or "Golden Horn."

Since it is located in an eminently seismic area and at the mouth of the bay, open to the immensity of the world's largest ocean, the Golden Gate Bridge had to be flexible. And flexible it is, capable of supporting side-to-side oscillations of 21 feet (7 m) and to buck vertically more than 10 feet (3 m). Its serpentine resistance has been sorely tested on many occasions; for example, when ocean storms hit the coast with gusts of wind not rarely in excess of 70 mph (110 km/h). In 1985 the roadbed was completely rebuilt and the cement was replaced with orthotropic steel plate decking, a lighter, tougher, more elastic material that notably alleviates the stress on the bridge's cables and towers.

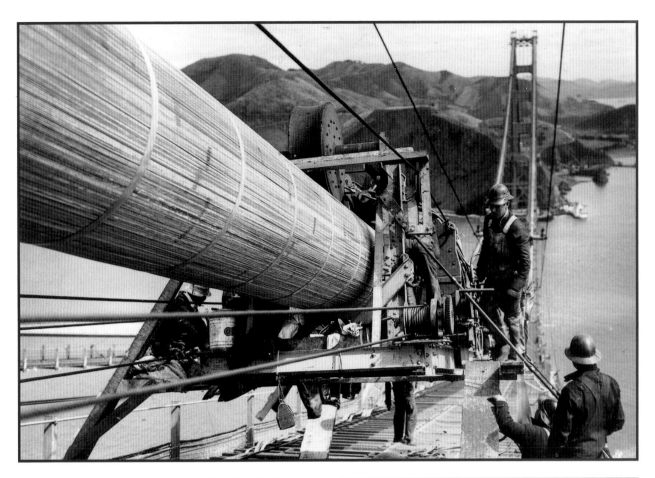

On these pages, two period photographs of the Golden Gate Bridge under construction.

Bottom, right, the commemorative statue of the Chief Engineer of the Golden Gate Bridge project, Joseph B. Strauss.

With its 4200 ft (1280 m) center span, the Golden Gate Bridge held the world record for span length between pylons until 1964, when it was dethroned by New York's Verrazzano Narrows Bridge.

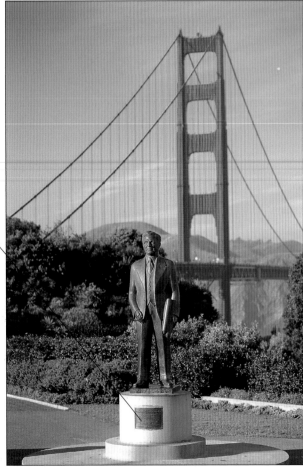

The Man Who Built the Bridge

"Here at the Golden Gate is the
Eternal Rainbow that he conceived
And set to form, a promise indeed
That the race of man shall Endure unto the Ages."

BUILDING THE GOLDEN GATE BRIDGE

The Marin Tower, completed in 1934, rests on the coast.

Height of the roadbed with respect to sea level: 276 ft (72.6 m).

The bases of the towers are strengthened by internal steel reinforcements.

The water under the centerpoint of the span is more than 295 ft (90 m) deep.

Fender, with warning lights for passing vessels.

The Golden Gate Bridge in Numbers

Address: Highway 101 between San Francisco and Marin Counties
Length of center span: 4200 ft, 1280 m
Total suspended length: 6450 ft, 1960 m
Total length: 9052 ft, 2743 m
Length of each carrying cable: 7659 ft, 2320m
Height of towers: 750 ft, 227m
Initial cost at time of construction: 33 million US dollars
Inauguration: 27 May 1937, opened to pedestrian traffic only;
28 May 1937, opened to vehicular traffic.
Average daily users: 125,000 vehicles
Number of lanes: 6 (reversible)
Toll: $ 5
Maintenance staff: 17 steel workers and 38 painters

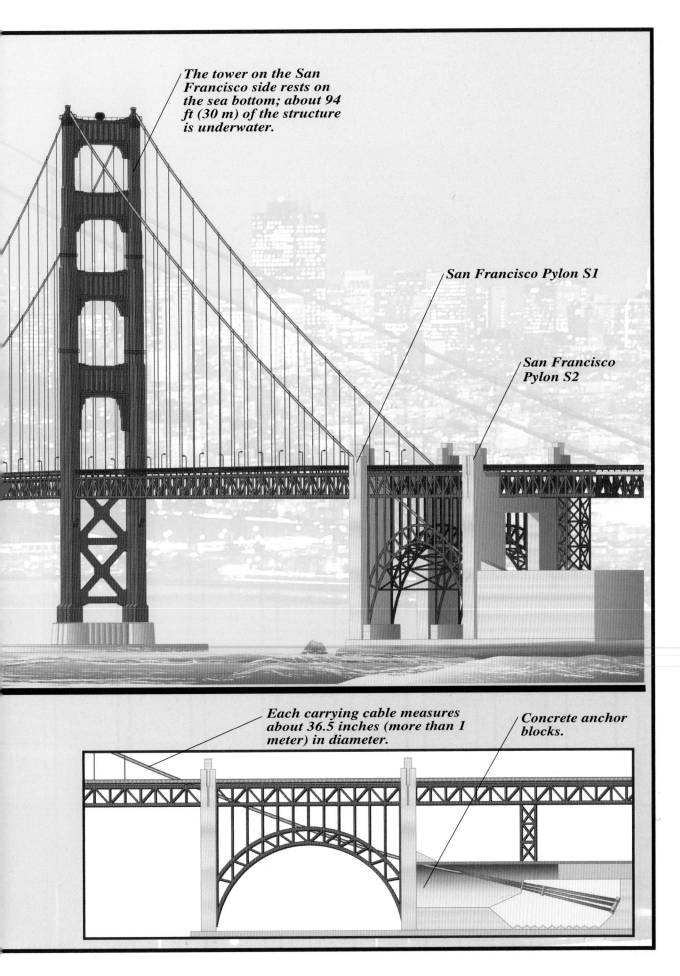

The tower on the San Francisco side rests on the sea bottom; about 94 ft (30 m) of the structure is underwater.

San Francisco Pylon S1

San Francisco Pylon S2

Each carrying cable measures about 36.5 inches (more than 1 meter) in diameter.

Concrete anchor blocks.

19

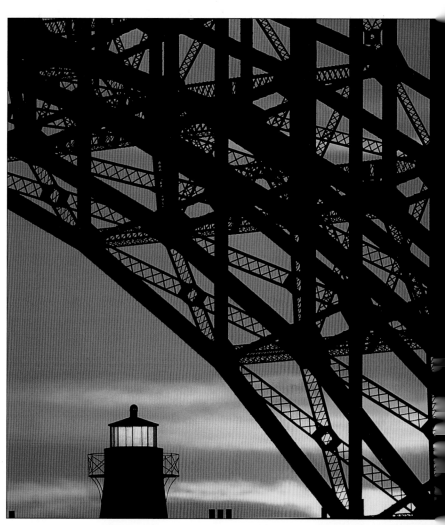

When the Golden Gate Bridge was completed in 1937, it was the longest continuous bridge span in the world.

UNION SQUARE

The bronze Victory *high above Union Square.*

*T*he Union Square neighborhood is San Francisco's most famous shopping center and—with annual sales topping $1 billion—is second only to New York as the nation's most illustrious retail district. The area is a Shangri-la of shopping where you can buy just about anything. There are trendy fashion boutiques as well as legendary stalwarts of style like Hermès, Tiffany and Cartier. Chain outlets and colossal department stores abound featuring all the big names like Saks Fifth Avenue and Macy's, Nordstrom and Neiman-Marcus. Hotels, restaurants and art galleries fuel the voracious fires of commerce, and then there are the legions of sidewalk flower stands, colorful vendors that have lined the streets of **Union Square** since the late 1800s. At the heart of all this bustling consumerism is Union Square itself, a 2.6-acre manicured park that offers relief to weary shoppers and locals alike. The Square is named for the pro-Union rallies held here on the eve of the Civil War. Interestingly, the Square serves as the landscaped roof of a five-floor underground parking garage built in 1942, when it offered valet parking for shoppers. The center of the Square is marked by a granite column that commemorates the victory of Admiral Dewey's fleet at Manila Bay during the Spanish-American war. The face of the monument's bronze statue, **Victory**, was modeled after Mrs. Adolph de Bretteville Spreckels, the famed city benefactor. For well over a century the Square's meandering gardens and paths have been the city's premiere crossroads, a lively place to people-watch and absorb the sights and sounds of the city. All walks of life converge here daily, from street artists and musicians to chess players and panhandlers, from office workers, catching their breath to the city's famed white-gloved matrons doing their early morning shopping. Originally Union Square was not a shopping center at all. Quite the contrary, it was a focus of religious life, primarily for Jews and Protestants. After Jasper O'Farrell cleared the Square as a public space in 1847, no fewer than three Protestant churches lined the Square, and a fourth was less than a block away along with a Jewish temple. By the close of the nineteenth century, all but one of these places of worship had moved out of the neighborhood. In the latter part of the nineteenth century, Union Square was also recognized as the home and playground of the city's rich and mighty. Several private clubs sprung up along Post Street to cater to the city's social elite, many of whom lived conveniently nearby. Lined with Victorian mansions and townhouses, Sutter Street was the most fashionable and prestigious place of residence at that time. As the area became more crowded, however, the aristocracy moved west to even grander domains in Pacific Heights. Businesses swooped in to convert these palatial private houses into shops and stores, and thus one of the nation's retail capitals was born. Today Union Square is marked by several notable structures. To the west stands the **Westin St. Francis Hotel**, as visually commanding today as it was when it was constructed in 1904 by Charles T. Crocker. Designed by Bliss & Faville, this skyscraper hotel drastically altered the complexion of the neighborhood and boldly heralded the arrival of commerce to Union Square. Although the hotel suffered severe earthquake damage in 1906, its steel-frame construction saved the building from annihilation. When it was rebuilt in 1908, the St. Francis had 750 rooms, more than any other hotel on the Pacific coast. The hotel was expanded again in later years, so the building now has 1,200 rooms and spans the entire park block. In addition, there are seven restaurants on the premises, and the Grand Ballroom holds more than 1,500 people. In 1972 William Pereira Associates added a tower and exterior elevators that offer an impressive view of the city. The department stores on the Square are revered more for fashionable merchandise than innovative architecture, but for the most part the buildings do accommodate their setting—a statement that cannot be made for most retail monoliths. Designed by Hellmuth, Obata & Kassabaum in 1981, **Saks Fifth Avenue** commands the northwest corner of Union Square. While not as bold visually as the New York City flagship, the building's round corners and subtle colors distinguish the exterior. Inside the architecture is less successful, as the jumble of escalators diminishes all sense of space.

Union Square is the heart of the city's most important shopping district.

The atrium of Neiman-Marcus on Stockton Street. Bottom, Maiden Lane.

Following page, from top to bottom: a portrait of Frank Lloyd Wright, the designer of Circle Gallery; an image of the Crocker Galleria's glass promenade.

NEIMAN-MARCUS

B uilt by Philip Johnson and John Burgee in 1982 on the southeast corner of Union Square, Neiman-Marcus rose at the expense of an old favorite, the City of Paris general store, which had occupied the spot since 1896. The superb four-story rotunda of City of Paris, designed by Bakewell and Brown in 1908, is in fact housed within the dramatic red granite and glass façade of Neiman-Marcus. The rotunda has beautiful belle époque plaster flourishes; the subtle, white and gold stained-glass canopy depicts a ship at sea—the symbol of Paris, France. In all, the preservation of the old store is perhaps the finest attribute of the new.

MAIDEN LANE

O n the east side of Union Square is the entrance to Maiden Lane, formerly and infamously known as Morton Street. Until the earthquake and fire of 1906 cleaned out the cribs with Biblical vengeance, Morton Street was lined with prostitutes and bordellos. The whole street was a red-light district with prostitutes flaunting their wares and soliciting passersby from open windows. Astoundingly, this few block stretch averaged almost two murders a week. Eventually the area's budding commerce transformed this street as well, and local entrepreneurs managed to change the street's name to convey the new ethic. Today Maiden Lane is a lovely pedestrian walkway lined with chic boutiques and fancy restaurants with outdoor dining in nice weather. It certainly has come a long way.

Frank Lloyd Wright

O ne of America's most celebrated architects, Wright (1869-1959) apprenticed in Chicago—in the late 1800's—with the sketcher J. L. Silsbee, doing architectural detailing, and then with the prestigious architectural firm of Dankmar Adler and Louis Sullivan.

His vast portfolio ranges from the "Prairie houses" of the early 1900's, typical one-family homes skillfully inserted into natural environment, to the "Usonian houses" of the 1930's, in which he made use of new materials (for example, reinforced concrete) and new structural criteria; the Kaufmann House at Bear Run is a well-known example. The Taliesin West complex near Phoenix splendidly synthesizes Wright's conception of architecture. Wright began experimenting with circular structures in his seventies: the famous Solomon R. Guggenheim Museum (1959) in New York is the most famous, but his **Circle Gallery** in San Francisco predates it by ten years.

THE CIRCLE GALLERY

A t 140 Maiden Lane is the outstanding Circle Gallery designed by **Frank Lloyd Wright** in 1949. Formerly a crystal and china shop known as V.C. Morris—the name is still visible in Wright's handsomely chiseled lettering—this building is one of the city's greatest architectural achievements. As in all of Wright's works, form and function are closely allied in the structure's architectural concepts: the circular design motifs used throughout the building gave a wink to the shapes of the plates and saucers displayed within. Circles appear subtly in every detail of the building, from the grand scheme of the architecture to the minute considerations of the furnishings. Though the original building dates from 1911, Wright's renovation did not leave much trace of the former structure. Outside, Wright emphasized the play of light on the brickwork and the ornately detailed archway at the opening. Lights were placed along the façade's ornate molding, and the sidewalk at the entrance—now cemented over—even featured a semi-circle of lights under glass. Wright fans should appreciate the red square tile in the lower left corner of the façade that bears the architect's signature. Inside, the spiral ramp leading to the upper floor was one of the precursors to Wright's design of the Guggenheim Museum in New York City. It rises gently to the skylighted ceiling, again emphasizing the nuance of light and space. Although the gallery displays contemporary art, don't forget to notice what's left of Wright's original walnut furniture, recognizable—of course—for its circle motif.

CROCKER GALLERIA

W hen Crocker Bank built its towering pink granite headquarters in 1982, it included a glass-roofed, barrel-vaulted shopping arcade, the Crocker Galleria. The thirty-eight story tower, designed by Skidmore, Owings & Merrill, has since been renamed Telesis Tower, but the Galleria remains.

The three-level Galleria is modeled after the enormous Galleria Vittorio Emanuele in Milan, Italy. Although much smaller, the Crocker has an expansive central plaza under the vaulted skylight roof and over fifty stores and restaurants. Fashion boutiques include such fabulously chic as Gianni Versace and Ralph Lauren.

SAN FRANCISCO SHOPPING CENTRE

Another shopping attraction in the Union Square neighborhood is the San Francisco Shopping Centre, a ten-level vertical shopping mall with over one hundred shops, cafés and restaurants. The Centre looks quite impressive—even along this block of stately neoclassical buildings. The façade is appropriately cast in gray granite, and the roofline is recessed to give the building a loftier aspect and to allow more sunlight into Hallidie Plaza across the street. The atrium at the pinnacle is covered with a large steel and glass dome that opens when the weather is good.

Inside, the building is equally impressive. The top four levels of the Centre were converted into a spectacular **Nordstrom** department store in 1988 by architecture firm Whisler-Patri. Besides sumptuous merchandise, one of the main attractions here is the country's first semi-spiral escalators. Designed by Mitsubishi, these three pairs of curved escalators wind along the building's central well up to the domed roof.

The Centre also boasts another interesting feature that is discreetly hidden from public view: two sixty-foot-long elevators lift thirty-ton trucks from street level to the building's down floor, making deliveries a cinch.

A vertiginous view of the Nordstrom department store, located in the SF Shopping Centre.

Two images of the Hallidie Building, named after Andrew Hallidie, the inventor of the cable car.

HALLIDIE BUILDING

Across Sutter Street is the impressive Hallidie Building, designed by Willis Polk in 1917 and believed to feature the world's first glass curtain wall façade, which is projected a few feet beyond the reinforced concrete structure. For that alone, the Hallidie is San Francisco's most important building, setting an historic precedent in the annals of modern urban architecture. Built for the University of California, the building was named after Andrew Hallidie, inventor of the cable car and a university regent.

The façade is further enhanced by beautiful, Regency-inspired fire escapes and an imposing Venetian Gothic cornice.

POWELL STREET CABLE-CAR TURNAROUND

in, unload, get turned around manually by the cable car conductors and then dutifully load up for the next voyage. The whole process is charmingly awkward.

The first cable-car voyage was launched in 1873, when Scottish inventor Andrew Hallidie guided his car along Clay Street, navigating five treacherously hilly blocks en route to Chinatown. Hallidie, who had previously been a mine-cable engineer during California's Gold Rush, decided to implement the cable-car system after having witnessed a brutal accident involving a horse car on one of the city's notorious hills. Quickly after their inaugural run, cable cars transformed the city. They represented a safe and efficient means of transportation. Neighborhoods that were previously deemed unsuitable for living suddenly became quite hospitable with the new cable car system. The network peaked just before the 1906 earthquake, when there were almost 600 cars and 110 miles of track.

One of the hubs of the city's historic cable-car lines is the Powell Street turntable at Hallidie Plaza, where a lengthy line of tourists is always waiting to hop aboard. The wait can be a long one, but usually there is an array of street performers there to entertain. When the cable cars arrive at the turntable, the pit-stop is quite entertaining in itself. The cars come

The Powell Street Cable Car turntable at Hallidie Plaza is a great tourist attraction.

Opposite, cable cars offer exquisite views of the city and the bay.

Cable Car Museum

The Cable Car Museum is a spectacle of mechanical ingenuity.

The mighty engines that pull the city's cable cars along their routes are found in the Cable Car Museum, which still hums with power all day long. The barn houses the mechanisms that make the cable cars go: purring engines power huge, fourteen-foot sheaves that wind the cables, pulling the cars along their tracks. Being inside the museum and watching the dynamo churn feels like being inside an enormous clock.

The barn was first constructed in 1887 and then rebuilt in 1906 after the quake badly damaged the structure. When the cable-car system was renovated during the 1980s, the barn was reinforced but the exterior was left alone.

An underground viewing room shows how the cables loop in and out below street level.

The museum also houses three vintage cable cars as well as displays that describe the cars' grip and braking mechanisms in full detail. Photographs and scale models document all the cars that ever grappled a San Francisco hill.

The earthquake and the ensuing fire did extensive damage, however. Many lines were not rebuilt, and others were replaced with electric cable cars. With the invention and proliferation of the automobile, the cable car system dwindled dramatically over the next fifty years.

In an effort to stem the rapid deterioration of the lines, the city voted to preserve the cable car system in 1955. Nine years later, San Francisco's cable cars became the first moving National Historic Landmarks in the country. In 1984, a massive two-year, $60 million renovation was completed that again rejuvenated the cable cars. The entire system was overhauled. The cars' new seats and wheels and shiny coat of maroon, blue and gold paint were only the most obvious renovations. The tracks and cable vaults were replaced with deeper grooved rails and more flexible

Two period photographs of the early cable cars. Right, a historical cable car with the inventor of this means of public transport, Andrew Hallidie, seated in the front row.

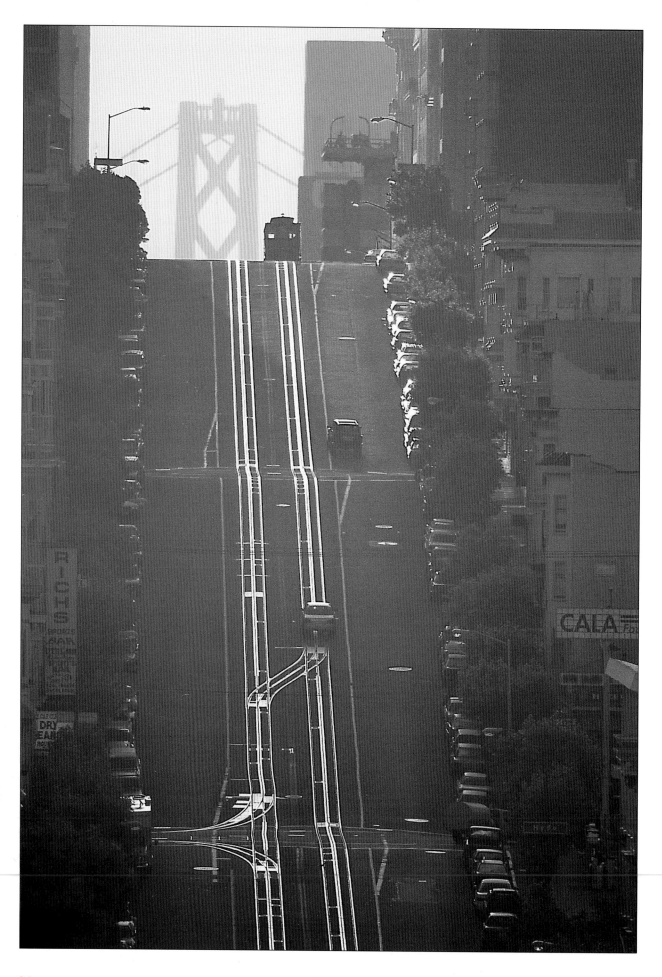

curves, and the pulleys and depression beams that guide each cable were restored. Many of the cable-car routes were redirected to flow with automobile traffic. The renovation task was enormous, but today the system shines in all its historic glory. There are forty-four cars in the fleet today, with as many as twenty-seven climbing the hills at any given time. The city's ten miles of track are divided into three separate lines, of which the Powell-Hyde Line is said to offer the most panoramic views of the city as well as the most exciting curves. The faint of heart and stomach shouldn't worry about the curves, however, because each six-ton car travels at a steady, non-threatening 9.5 or 8,5 miles an hour. Each car is pulled along by a cable beneath the street that moves by the turning of an enormous, fourteen-foot wheel housed in a car barn. If you want to see how all this works, the historic **Cable Car Barn** at Washington and Mason streets was completely renovated and restored to its original appearance in the 1984 refurbishment. Each wheel and cable is constantly in motion, so the cable-car operator starts and stops the car by mechanically gripping and releasing the cable. The system seems almost too simple for our hurly-burly world, but thirteen million passengers climb on the cable cars each year—that's almost 36,000 a day!

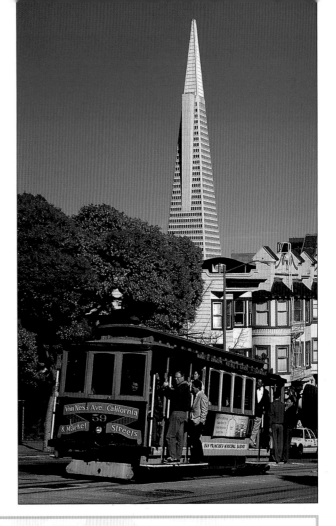

Half the fun of going to San Francisco is a cable car ride.

Opposite, a suggestive image of a cable car with the Bay Bridge in the distance.

The Theater District

The six or seven blocks west of Union Square comprise what is commonly known as San Francisco's Theater District. San Franciscans have been ardent theater supporters since the days of the Gold Rush, when miners were known to shower stage starlets with bags of gold dust. Though in many ways cut off from the cultural milieu of the other world capitals, San Franciscans were remarkably sophisticated even in the early years. With great fanfare, the city's first opera house opened in 1851. **Lotta's Fountain**, located at the intersection of Geary, Kearny and Market streets, stands to this day as a testament of the city's lasting appreciation of the performing arts. The fountain commemorates the career of actress Lotta Crabtree, who began her career in San Francisco as a dancer during the Gold Rush.

During the 1920s, vaudeville acts set up shop in the Union Square area and constructed lavish theaters in the process. In fact the best of these theaters remain today, with their ornate fixtures and elaborately carved fittings well preserved. Several of these theaters can rival any house on New York City's Broadway in terms of visual opulence as well as outstanding production. The **Curran**, **Golden Gate** and **Orpheum Theaters** all seat up to 2,000 people and receive top-notch musicals directly from the stages of New York and London. The **American Conservatory Theater (ACT)**, one of the most highly respected repertory companies in the country, has recently returned to the 1,300-seat **Geary Theater**, which underwent major refurbishment after the 1989 Loma Prieta earthquake. For six years after the quake, ACT held performances at two other medium-sized theaters in the area, **Theater on the Square** and **Stage Door Theater**, both renowned for more experimental productions. The avant-garde is also well represented at the nearby **Marines Memorial Theater** and the **New Conservatory Theater Center**.

Lotta's Fountain.
Isadora Duncan was born at #501 Taylor Street.

FINANCIAL DISTRICT

San Francisco's Financial District is as powerful commercially as it is elegant visually. One of the four largest business centers in the United States, the Financial District rises dramatically on the horizon as one approaches the city, as some 225,000 commuters do every day to get to work. The natural terrain of the city gives the downtown area an ethereal aspect, that of the proverbial city on the hill, a financial mecca indeed. Despite its commercial power, the Financial District is actually quite compact, designed on a very human scale. All points of commerce are within easy walking distance. "Wall Street West" is home to some of the largest corporations in the world, including Chevron, Transamerica, Bechtel, Pacific Gas & Electric, Bank of America and Levi Strauss, an international favorite. Despite the presence of these financial giants, the vast majority of businesses are small, with fewer than ten employees. Not surprisingly, the proximity of Silicon Valley has made the Financial District one of the world leaders in technology and communications development. The landscape of the Financial District was drastically altered by the Gold Rush of 1849 and the rise of the "instant city," which transformed San Francisco from a quiet port of less than one thousand people to a major metropolis of over twenty thousand. Amazingly, much of the District was once covered by the San Francisco Bay. Montgomery Street was the eastern frontier of the city, poised on what was known as Yerba Buena Cove. Inadvertently and over many years, the city expanded eastward: an ocean wall was built in the Bay to facilitate the unloading of cargo ships during the Gold Rush, while at the same time Yerba Buena Cove was slowly being graded by overuse. The arrival of thousands of ships depleted the shores of the Cove; where necessary, mud flats were filled in with sand and dirt taken from nearby hills. Over the course of a few decades, the Cove was entirely covered with landfill and eventually joined the sea wall. Many of the buildings we see on the eastern shore today, therefore, were built on land claimed from the sea. Within a few years of the Gold Rush and before the Cove could be filled in, however, Montgomery Street was the focus of the city's finances. Because they were equipped to weigh and buy the gold dust being unloaded at port, waterfront shop keepers became bankers almost overnight. Soon Montgomery Street was lined with banks, and the surrounding area attracted luxury retail merchants. In 1854 the Gold Rush went bust in a fit of rash speculation. The Panic of Black Friday ensued, forcing many banks to close. Nevertheless, the Financial District was born. In the 1890s the Victorian city was transformed by the iron- and steel-frame, brick-clad skyscrapers that arose in the Financial District. The **Chronicle Building** at Market and Kearny streets became San Francisco's first skyscraper in 1889. This home of the San Francisco Chronicle was designed by the Chicago firm of Burnham and Root. Although the building still stands, unfortunately the façade lost most of its charm when it was "modernized" in 1962. Thankfully, a few blocks away on Montgomery Street, Burnham and Root's **Mills Building** appears today much as it did upon construction in 1891. Its Romanesque Revival façade retains the nascent glory of the

California skyscraper. The proliferation of skyscrapers at the turn of the century greatly expanded downtown San Francisco and drastically altered the look of the whole city. When the earthquake struck in 1906, there were over twenty steel-frame skyscrapers in the Financial District alone. Although fires gutted the insides of many skyscrapers, the steel frames resisted fire damage and made rebuilding possible. When the city was reconstructed in the following years, the pre-fire skyscrapers remained as models. The

A night view of Financial District.

Following pages: the Financial District with the SF-Oakland Bay Bridge.

rebuilt city, therefore, had a remarkable architectural coherence. In the mid-1920s another building boom swept through the Financial District, again changing the skyline. The new wave of skyscrapers were taller and—with towers receding from the street—appeared to soar, indeed. The **Shell Building** on Bush Street and the Miller and Pleuger-designed **450 Sutter Street** are the best examples of this architectural era, which ended soundly with the Stock Market Crash of 1929. Not until the 1960s would the downtown area undergo any major architectural projects, and then it was only to produce sterile plazas and cold office towers, a tradition that would continue for years to come.

TRANSAMERICA PYRAMID

The Transamerica Pyramid has become San Francisco's signature landmark. In both size and majesty, nothing dominates the city's skyline quite like the Pyramid. At 853 feet, the Pyramid is the city's most towering skyscraper—only the Sutro Television Tower atop Twin Peaks is a taller structure. The Pyramid is visible at points throughout the city and, indeed, from across the Bay as well. Although the building is for the most part universally embraced today, it has not enjoyed such acclaim for long. In fact, when the building was completed in 1972 after almost three years of construction, it caused great controversy for being too big, too corporate, too flashy for quiet San Francisco.

Designed by Los Angeles architect William Pereira and Associates, the Pyramid climbs forty-eight stories. Originally, Transamerica chairman John Beckett had wanted the building to soar to one thousand feet and fifty-five stories. The plan was downsized after broad civic protests. As it is, the building's curtain walls are made up of three-thousand quartz-aggregate concrete panels that weigh three-and-a-half tons each. The concrete-and-steel foundation, sunk more than fifty feet into the ground, weighs more than 30,000 tons. The structure is topped by a hollow, illuminated, 212-foot spire. All together, the project cost almost $45 million. Today the Pyramid is home to more than fifty firms, which in turn employ more than 1,500 people. Tourists and city residents alike enjoy the changing art exhibits in the lobby, and the observation area on the 27th floor provides excellent northern views of such landmarks as Coit Tower, Alcatraz and the Golden Gate Bridge. Directly to the east is **Transamerica Redwood Park**, a half-acre landscaped park designed by Tom Galli. This miniature forest includes eighty redwood trees transplanted from the Santa Cruz Mountains. The Pyramid is the eponymously-named home office of Transamerica, which was founded by A.P. Giannini in 1928 as a bank holding company. Today the business is an enormous corporate conglomerate with 11,000 employees worldwide and assets estimated at more than $32 billion. The building site, located at the end of Columbus Avenue on the fringe of North Beach's cafe culture, was bought by Transamerica for $8 million in 1969. The location itself has an interesting history, having once been the site of the city's prime literary and artistic crossroads. The Montgomery Block building, affectionately known as the Monkey Block, was built in 1853 and stood here for over a century. For decades the building was the largest west of the Mississippi, and perhaps the most important meeting place in the West as well. Though intended as offices for prominent businesses, the building was eventually taken over by writers and newspapermen. At one point the building was more of a live-in dormitory for bohemian poets, artists and political radicals. Mark Twain met a fireman named Tom Sawyer here in the basement steam baths. George Sterling, Maynard Dixon, Ambrose Pierce, Bret Harte and Joaquin Miller were among those who frequently pulled up a stool at the bar. Sun Yat-sen, who would later overthrow China's Manchu Dynasty, published *Young China* from his second-floor office here.

San Francisco is a city of contrasts. Here the Transamerica Pyramid confronts a lovely Victorian.

The miniature forest of Transamerica Redwood Park; opposite, the iconic Transamerica Pyramid.

JACKSON SQUARE HISTORICAL DISTRICT

Designated the city's first historic district, Jackson Square was the only downtown area left standing after the 1906 earthquake. Most of these brick buildings date back to the 1850s and give an idea of what the city looked like during the Gold Rush and the early days of the "instant city." What remains of the district, bounded by Montgomery and Sansome streets and Jackson and Washington streets, constitutes what was the city's original financial district, which then became the city's most nefarious prostitution quarters.

In San Francisco's earliest days, both commerce and retail were centered in Portsmouth Square and what is now the Jackson Square Historical District. Montgomery Street bordered the Bay at Yerba Buena Cove, and there the city had decided to set up shop. The Gold Rush and the subsequent influx of thousands of miners and traders to the city changed all that. The city grew twenty-fold almost overnight, and what had been the focus of the city's financial life suddenly got a new address. The physical transformation of the city, the expansion of the eastern frontier into Yerba Buena Cove, changed where the city did business. Commercial interests moved to where the money was. The Gold Rush trade was happening along the expanding shipping ports to the south and east. The city's present-day Financial District was born then and there, leaving Jackson Square to another fate. As businesses began to move out of the Jackson Square area, a new element began to move in. Gold Rush fever brought thousands of men westward seeking fame and fortune. Most of them didn't have much luck finding

either, and all of them were lonely and desperate for companionship. They tended to drift to San Francisco for comfort, and the city was all too eager to please. The area around Jackson Square, in fact, became known as the **Barbary Coast**—named after an infamous port in Northern Africa—because of its boundless perversion and wickedness. Drinking, gambling and prostitution became big business.

Pacific Street was the Barbary Coast's main thoroughfare and became known as "Terrific Pacific." A line of bordellos, raunchy saloons and gambling halls stretched six blocks from the waterfront. Certain stretches earned titles like "Murderer's Corner", "Battle Row", and "Dead Man's Alley". In 1908 The Dash opened at Pacific and Kearny and became the city's first gay bar. Lawlessness reigned and violence and debauchery were its henchmen. Casual death was almost as commonplace as casual sex. The lure of the Barbary Coast was so great that ship captains had to "Shanghai" prospective sailors in waterfront bars. The practice involved knocking out bar customers with a spiked drink and then carrying his unconscious body to a ship, on which he would have to work his passage to some distant port.

For almost sixty years the Barbary Coast partied on, to the moral outrage of many of the city's governors. In April of 1906 the earthquake and fire destroyed much of the Coast, although amazingly Jackson Square itself was spared. Mired in six square miles of smoking embers, the Square stood unscathed, the only downtown survivor. So the debauchery continued, and only in 1917 did civic decree put a damper on the festivities. Even so, the newly-coined International Settlement endured, in more modest terms, until the 1950s.

Today, the elegant, tree-lined streets of the Barbary Coast are thoroughly gentrified. The area is now known as Jackson Square, although no square is to be found. Designers, architects and antique dealers occupy many of these historic brick houses and cast-iron office buildings. The east side of the **700 block of Montgomery Street** has several of these notable buildings, as does the **400 block of Jackson Street** around the corner. **Gold Street** has the most well-preserved stretch of 1850's architecture; the **Bank of Lucas, Tuner & Company** at the western end was constructed in 1853 and managed by William Tecumseh Sherman, who would later burn Atlanta as a Union general in the Civil War.

Gold Street, an emblematic byway in the Barbary Coast area.

Typical brick buildings in the Jackson Square Historical District.

MERCHANT'S EXCHANGE BUILDING

The Merchant's Exchange Building.

Several buildings in the Financial District are renowned for their fine, intricate masonry. The Royal Insurance Building and the Pacific Gas and Electric Company are among the most beautiful.

As one of the original steel-frame buildings in San Francisco and as a survivor of the 1906 earthquake, the Merchant's Exchange is one of the city's most important office buildings. Designed by Willis Polk of the Chicago architecture firm D.H. Burnham in 1903, the Exchange was one the prototypes for the post-quake building boom of the early twentieth century. Today the Exchange also happens to house some of the city's finest public art.

The building's classical façade is given a focus by the stately twin columns around the entrance. Inside, the marble lobby features ornately designed elevator doors and wonderful model ships.

The skylight above creates a Pantheon-esque effect. The lobby leads to the entrance of the **Grain Exchange Hall,** once the commercial center of the entire West Coast, and today the office of First Interstate Bank. In days of yore, when shipping was the city's primary commerce, a look-out posted on the roof of the Exchange would herald the arrival of ships to the traders and businessmen gathered in the great hall below. Although primitive in means, the bustling atmosphere was not unlike the floor of our modern-day stock exchanges. Constructed like the portico of an ancient Greek temple, the Grain Exchange opens onto a hall hung with a series of large oil paintings by marine painters William Coulter and Nils Hagerup. Coulter is renowned for his detailed depictions of turn-of-the-century ports and sailing vessels. The collection here, painted around 1910, focuses on San Francisco's shipping industry and is considered among his best work.

Paintings like *Arrived, All Well* and *War Time* give wonderful perspectives of this newly-born capital of the West.

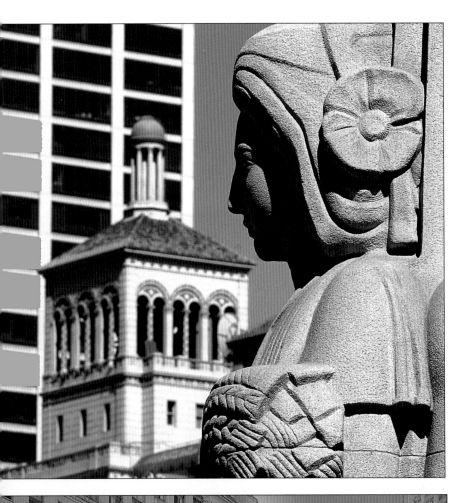

PACIFIC COAST STOCK EXCHANGE

Outside of New York, the Pacific Coast Stock Exchange is the country's largest stock market. Financially, the Exchange is the heart and soul of the district's bustling commerce: through the open front door, visitors can see the frantic trading on the floor. Architecturally, however, the building presents a somewhat awkward mix of classical and Moderne styles. Originally designed by Cleveland architect J. Milton Dyer in 1915 to house the U.S. Subtreasury, the Exchange building has a complex history. After the Stock market Crash of 1929, the government moved out and the San Francisco Stock Exchange moved in. Dyer's classical façade, that of a somber granite temple adorned with a Doric colonnade, was recommissioned by Miller and Pfleuger in 1930 to give the building a more contemporary look. The overhaul included adding Moderne bas-relief motifs to the building's cornice and massive sculptures, designed by Ralph Stackpole, along the entryway. To the right is Stackpole's *Man and His Inventions*, to the left *Mother Earth*. Miller and Pfleuger were also commissioned to design the twelve-story granite office tower behind the Exchange. Again Stackpole was called upon to create a monumental high-relief carving, *The Progress of Man*, over the entrance. The lobby is equally muscular, bedecked with black marble and a geometric, gold-leaf ceiling. Upstairs is the City Club, a private watering hole reserved for members of the stock exchange. Along the way in the club's two-story stairwell is Diego Rivera's superb mural *Allegory of California*, which depicts California as bounteous, life-bearing Mother.

On this page, the Pacific Coast Stock Exchange, the largest stock market in the US outside of New York.

Buildings and skyscrapers in the Financial District.

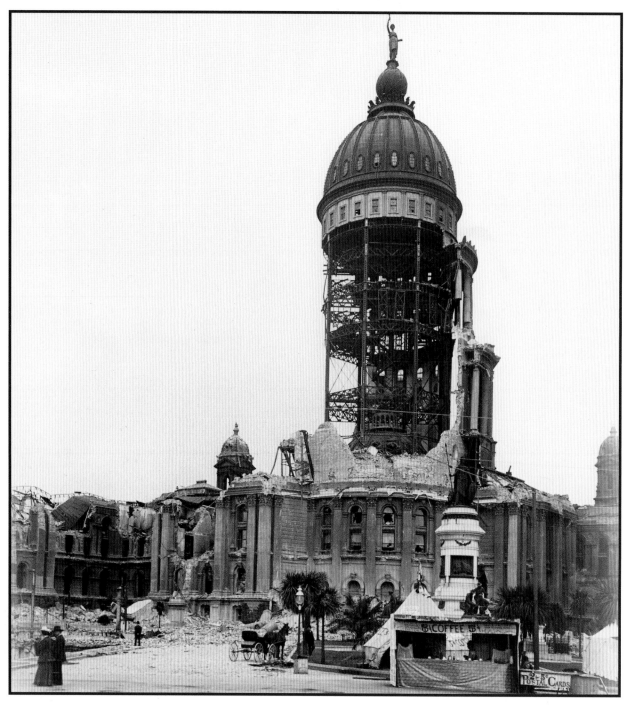

The old city hall destroyed by the 1906 earthquake and, on the facing page, the majestic facade of City Hall in the Civic Center.

On pages 48-49: aerial view of San Francisco's Civic Center.

CIVIC CENTER

San Francisco's Civic Center is renowned as the finest collection of Beaux Arts buildings in the United States. One man can be credited with much of the Civic Center's brilliance: Daniel Burnham, the Chicago architect commissioned in 1904 to design the city's master plan. Burnham, along with his young assistant, Willis Polk, were called upon by former Mayor James Phelan and several other prominent city benefactors to remedy the city's blight of unattractive architecture.

Although political scandal and the catastrophe of 1906 delayed construction of the Civic Center until after Burnham's death, the city wisely followed his recommendations and created a wonderful public space. Mayor "Sunny" Jim Rolph was the man who actually carried out the plans for the Civic Center. He was a stalwart supporter of City Beautiful principles, and under his guidance San Francisco achieved one of the world's finest civic centers.

CITY HALL

Designed in 1915 by prominent Bay Area architect Arthur Brown, City Hall is the centerpiece of the Civic Center and the grandest public space in the city. It is a monument imbued with civic pride—not only for its beauty, but also for the hope it fostered during a tumultuous era in the city's history. On April 18, 1906, an earthquake shook the city and leveled the old City Hall, which stood where the Main Public Library is today. An estimated 8.25 on the Richter scale—ten times more powerful than any other to hit the city before or since—the quake of 1906 killed 674 people and left 250,000 homeless. The catastrophe consumed 28,000 buildings, and property damages alone totaled $400 million. The city was in shambles and desperate for leadership. For years city government had been thwarted by scandal and corruption. After the catastrophe, reform-minded voters and politicians alike united to clean up the ruined municipality—inside and out. Corrupt city bosses were brought to justice: Abe Ruef pleaded guilty to extortion and was sentenced to fourteen years in San Quentin; ex-Mayor Schmitz was found guilty of twenty-seven counts graft and bribery. Construction of the $8.8 million City Hall, therefore, symbolized the dawning of a new political era, one led for almost twenty years by Republican mayor and future governor James Rolph, Jr. So large were Rolph's contributions to the city, upon his death in 1934 he was buried under City Hall's majestic dome, the finest building constructed during the glorious City Beautiful era. Brown's design won the $25,000 competition for City Hall, beating out almost eighty other entries. His Ecole des Beaux-Arts training in Paris is evident in the building's French Renaissance style. Other former students of the Ecole des Beaux-Arts included Jean Louis Bourgeois, who designed the interiors, and Henri Crenier, who created the vast, ornate array of sculptures. The building's huge lead and copper dome was modeled after St. Peter's Basilica in Rome. The dome itself is over 301 feet tall, rising three feet higher than that of the nation's capital. While the building has a sober, gray granite façade ornamented with stately Doric columns, the interior is much more lavish. The ceiling of the rotunda is decorated with a cartouche depicting a ship at sea. Exuberant Corinthian columns accent pink Tennessee marble floors and ornate, Indiana sandstone walls. A radiant sunburst clock hangs on one wall under an impressive sculpture of Father Time. The iron and bronze light fixtures and railings were made by Leo J. Myberg and represent some of the best Beaux Arts metalwork in the city. The first landing of the grand, flowing Baroque staircase is the city's most important public stage. In more recent history, City Hall was the site of the assassination of Mayor George Moscone and Supervisor Harvey Milk by disgruntled ex-supervisor Dan White on November 28, 1978. Supervisor Diane Feinstein was then named Mayor of the city, and her political career soared in the following years. In 1999, a major seismic upgrade and restoration of City Hall was completed under the guidance of Mayor Willie Brown.

LOUISE M. DAVIES SYMPHONY HALL

Designed by architects Skidmore, Owings & Merrill in 1980, the Louise M. Davies Symphony Hall is home to the top-notch San Francisco Symphony. From September through May, the Symphony packs the 2,743-seat building. The hall was named after arts patron Louise M. Davies, who donated $5 million to the $33 million project. The building's wrap-around glass and granite façade, which has more than a faint resemblance to a futuristic space station, had few supporters upon its completion. To make matters worse, for years the hall's acoustics were considered only mediocre.

In 1992—after years of deliberation—the hall completed a $10 million acoustical and architectural renovation. To improve sound quality, a new audio system was installed. Furthermore, the interior walls of the hall were resculptured—using state-of-the-art computer technology—to reflect sound better. Occasionally, the Davies showcases what is the nation's largest concert hall organ. Built by the Ruffatti brothers of Padua, Italy, the organ consists of 9,235 computer-aided pipes.

The sculpture gardens outside Louise M. Davies Symphony Hall.

The stately façade of War Memorial Opera House.

WAR MEMORIAL OPERA HOUSE

Opera is one of the primary social and cultural events in San Francisco. From the gala season-opener in September through December, the War Memorial Opera House is the place to be. Designed by Arthur Brown and dedicated to the memory of World War I soldiers, the lavish opera house opened on October 15, 1932. It was the first municipally financed opera house in the country and has since become the centerpiece of the city's Performing Arts Center. The building seats 3,176, and productions here are astounding, renowned the world over. One of the nation's oldest and most revered dance companies, the San Francisco Ballet, performs here as well, beginning its season right after the opera closes. Some interesting bits of trivia: it was here in 1945 that the first United Nations charter was signed; six years later, the Opera House was again the focus of international affairs when it hosted the signing of the peace treaty between the U.S. and Japan, officially ending World War II.

The San Francisco Public Library's "New Main"
building, opened on 18 April 1996.

NEW SAN FRANCISCO MAIN PUBLIC LIBRARY

The New San Francisco Main Public Library replaced the old one next door on Larkin Street in 1996. The new building, designed principally by New York City architect James Freed in a Postmodern-Deconstructivist style, is more than two and a half times the size of its Beaux-Arts predecessor. Ironically, George Kelham's 1916 library had replaced a previous library destroyed in the 1906 quake; Kelham's granite-clad building was itself badly damaged in the 1989 Loma Prieta earthquake and closed for several months. The Asian Art Museum—currently in Golden Gate Park—is now preparing to move into the old library building. The new library represents the culmination of several building projects funded in the prosperous 1980s and built in the early 1990s. Incredibly, $30 million was raised privately to furnish the interior, making this project the largest public/ private collaboration in the city's history. In a city of highly-educated, well-read citizens, it seems appropriate that this final project is a monumental library. The building is an interesting architectural amalgam. On one hand it seems to reflect the Civic Center's formal Beaux-Arts design, albeit with a Postmodern interpretation; on the other hand, it also appears to mimic the deconstructed, contemporary style of its neighbors on Grove and Hyde streets. Regardless, the building is quite striking and provocative to look at. A towering, five-story, glass-enclosed atrium dominates the building's interior. Like the old library, which was built around a monumental staircase, the new building also features a magnificent stairway that rises around the periphery of the atrium. The library houses more than a million books and is known for its collection of rare and handprinted editions—especially those printed in San Francisco. Within the library is the San Francisco History Room, the city's official archive. Both museum and research library, the History Room displays a rare collection of civic documents and photographs.

BILL GRAHAM CIVIC AUDITORIUM

The oldest building in the Civic Center, the Bill Graham Civic Auditorium was designed in Beaux-Arts style by architect John Galen Howard. The building was completed just before City Hall during the architectural renaissance that followed the earthquake and fire of 1906. French pianist Camille Saint Saens was the featured performer at the building's 1915 inauguration. Since then, the 7,000 seat auditorium has become one of the city's most important performance sites.

The building's name was changed in honor of Bill Graham—the famed rock music promoter who helped make San Francisco the epicenter of the country's 1960s cultural revolution—after his accidental and premature death in 1992. Graham opened such seminal '60s establishments as Winterland and the Fillmore East. In the process he brought such Rock & Roll legends as Jimi Hendrix and The Who to San Francisco. The cultural institution that is the Grateful Dead owes its existence in many ways to Bill Graham. He died in 1992, the most prolific promoter of all time.

"PAINTED LADIES"

On 18 April 1906, an earthquake measuring 8 on the Richter scale jolted San Franciscans out of bed before breakfast. the shock lasted only a minute, but its after-effects were devastating. Fires burned out of control for three days due to broken water mains, and entire city blocks were dynamited to check their spread. In the end, some 50,000 buildings were destroyed, and there were over 500 casualties. San Franciscans got up, quelled the fires, and rebuilt their city with their usual indomitable spirit.

A number of the Victorian homes that are precious city landmarks remained standing; others fell and were rebuilt.

A tribute to the carpenter's art, row upon row of these frame houses were erected in the late 1800s. Elements in an individual house may include gable and turret roofs, deep recesses and bay windows, stained glass, Ionic pediments, wooden filigree, and deep porches, all painted in strong clear colors with white trim.

Victorian yes, but above all eminently "San Franciscan."

Victorian Architecture

Decorative elements, like this medallion, add personal touches to the exteriors of the Victorians and contribute to creating the singular personality of each of these "ladies."

The entrance preceded by a colonnade and topped by a railed balcony is typical of the sober, Classical taste that prevails in the Italianate style homes – but there is no lack of other, more eccentric solutions. The bay windows, like many of the porches, draw on north-central European architecture.

Like other details, elaborate multicolored stained glass windows and skylights – whether in Art Nouveau or Gothic style – tell us much about the tastes of the first owners.

2615

Use of Classical-style architectural elements permitted inserting complex decorative panels in wood, plaster, or other materials, at times in clear contrast with the sober aspect of the construction as a whole.

In this example of a colonial **Queen Anne** home we note the characteristic element of this architectural genre, the round tower. In the other styles the tower, if there is one, is square or polygonal.

On some of the houses, typically sloping roofs top finely-worked cornices and, underneath, friezes reflecting all the imaginative flair of the decorator.

Besides the color schemes, which vary greatly, the Victorians are distinguished by the elaborate tympani, in a great variety of styles and motifs, that adorn the doors and windows.

VICTORIAN SAN FRANCISCO

One of the most spectacular and pleasant places to visit when you're in San Francisco is the Pacific Heights / Alamo Square area with its characteristic homes of the Victorian era. Almost 50,000 of these luxurious mansions were built by the upper middle class between 1850 and 1915, the city's boom years. A walk through the neighborhood is the ideal way to observe and enjoy their interesting— and at times bizarre— architectural detail. San Francisco's Victorian buildings are in three principal styles: *Italianate*, *Queen Anne*, and *Stick* or *Eastlake*.

2537-41 Washington. 1885.
Stick/Eastlake double House

Left, Pacific at the corner of Octavia. 1894. Colonial towered Queen Anne.

2509 Sacramento. 1886. Stick Style

The Italian style is set apart by its motifs inspired by the palaces of the Italian Renaissance, like the front doors framed by classical columns or the elongated windows.
The rounded turret and the recessed portico are instead distinguishing elements of the Queen Anne style.

Finally, the homes built of wooden slats with gingerbread trim are said to be in "stick" style. But quite often a single building will be a mix of one or more of these styles, as mixed are the colors of the exteriors: up to eleven in number.
And this being the case, what better nickname than "Painted Lady"!

Some Addressees

Mish House, 1153 Oak Street between Broderick and Divisadero Streets. Built in 1885 and winner of numerous awards.
Soencer House, 1080 Hughes Street at the corner of Baker Street. Built in 1895 by the architect Fred T. Rabin in Queen Anne style and known for its beautiful turret.
Alamo Square, one of San Francisco's most famous sites, was built up in 1894/95 in Queen Anne style.

3241 Sacramento. 1883. Stick Style

1347 McAllister. 1880.
French neo-Baroque

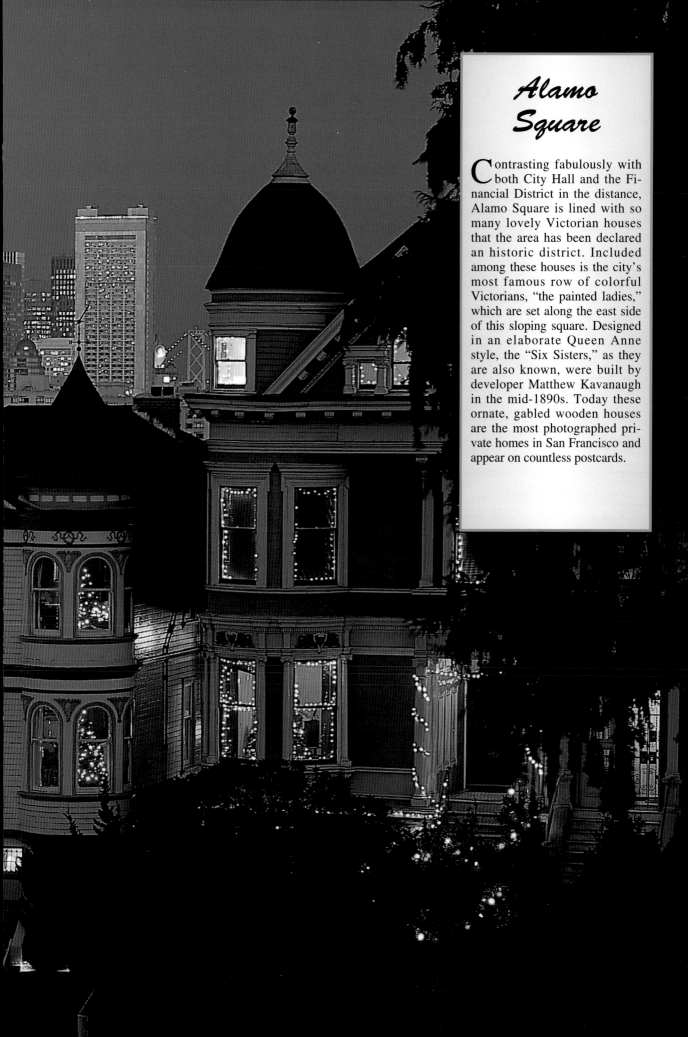

Alamo Square

Contrasting fabulously with both City Hall and the Financial District in the distance, Alamo Square is lined with so many lovely Victorian houses that the area has been declared an historic district. Included among these houses is the city's most famous row of colorful Victorians, "the painted ladies," which are set along the east side of this sloping square. Designed in an elaborate Queen Anne style, the "Six Sisters," as they are also known, were built by developer Matthew Kavanaugh in the mid-1890s. Today these ornate, gabled wooden houses are the most photographed private homes in San Francisco and appear on countless postcards.

PACIFIC HEIGHTS

Corner of Union Street and Buchanan Street and typical homes along Union Street.

San Francisco's most affluent neighborhood, Pacific Heights features some of the city's loveliest homes, many of which are splendid Victorians built in the wake of the 1906 temblor. The Heights became increasingly blue-blood with the introduction of the cable-car in 1873, when the city's affluent were lured away from the more established enclaves on Nob Hill. Fabulous monstrosities were built as neighbors competed to have the most opulent home. Along Van Ness Avenue especially, houses became quite decadent indeed.

The quake changed all that, of course, but Pacific Heights rose again. The exquisite views and natural beauty of the neighborhood simply could not be matched. Again the mansions were built, designed by such great architects as Willis Polk, Bernard Maybeck, Arthur Brown and George Applegarth. The mansions that grace the tree-lined streets that crest Pacific Heights offer some of the best views in the city of the bay and Golden Gate Bridge. To this day the neighborhood remains the wealthiest area in the city.

For years the Victorian houses along **Union Street** were some of the city's finest private homes. Today these old Victorians comprise one of the city's most chic commercial thoroughfares. Over 300 boutiques, restaurants, cafés and antique stores line Union Street. **Sacramento Street** and **Upper Fillmore Street** have also developed into major shopping arteries—not quite as trendy as Union Street, but not as touristy either. Here fabulous boutiques and upscale restaurants offer some of the city's finest pleasantries.

Spreckels Mansion — The single most spectacular house in the city, Spreckels Mansion was built for Adolph and Alma de Bretteville Spreckels in 1912. Adolph was one of many sons of sugar tycoon Claus Spreckels, and Alma—interestingly—was inspiration for the figure of Victory atop the Dewey Monument in Union Square. Their reinforced-concrete mansion, which occupies an entire block on Washington Street, was designed in Beaux Arts splendor by famed city architect George Applegarth. Applegarth would later build the Palace of the Legion of Honor for the Spreckels in the Presidio. Clad in white Utah limestone, the mansion overlooks Lafayette Park and is known as the "Pantheon of the West." It features several large, ornately detailed balconies and French windows. The façade is adorned with elaborate columns and beautiful *putti* statues. The gardens, fittingly, are extensive and well groomed. In 1990, romance novelist Danielle Steel bought the house for $8 million.

Spreckels Mansion, on the north side of Lafayette Park.

Octagon House — Built according to the once-popular superstition that eight-sided houses were lucky, Octagon House was built in 1861. At that time it was one of the city's five eight-sided buildings. The ground floor of Octagon House was altered when the house was moved from its original site across the street, but the upstairs remains the same. The National Society of Colonial Dames, an organization founded in 1891 to preserve the heritage of the country's colonial period, has occupied the house since 1951, when it began an extensive and thoughtful restoration. Since then the building has been converted into a museum that displays decorative arts from the Colonial and Federal periods.

Haas-Lilienthal House — Built in 1886 for wealthy merchant William Haas, the Haas-Lilienthal House is the only fully period-furnished Victorian house in the city open to the public. Designed in the Stick style with ornately carved wooden gables, elaborate ornamentation and a superb Queen Anne circular corner tower, Haas-Lilienthal House is an excellent model of the city's archetypal, nineteenth-century, upper-middle-class Victorian abode. The house was occupied by several generations of the Haas and Lilienthal families until 1972, when it was given to the Foundation for San Francisco's Architectural Heritage and opened as a museum. Inside the house is true to form—the furnishings preserve the time warp, showing just how far tastes have come in the past century.

The Octagon House, built in 1861.

The Haas-Lilienthal House, built in 1886.

Following pages, a row of Victorians.

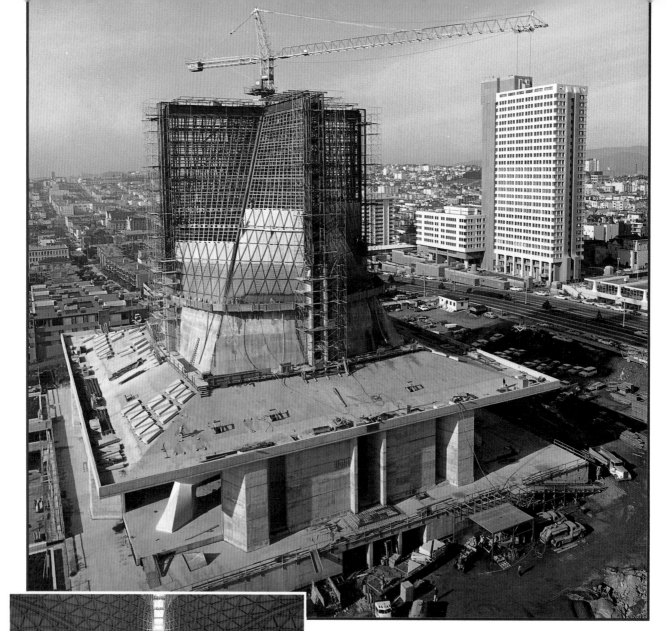

The construction of the ultramodern St. Mary's Cathedral, designed by Piero Belluschi and Pier Luigi Nervi.

The ceiling of St. Mary's Cathedral with its stained-glass cross.

ST. MARY'S CATHEDRAL

Commanding the summit of Cathedral Hill, St. Mary's was built in 1971 and has been one of the city's most distinctive landmarks ever since. Designed by architect **Pietro Belluschi** and engineer **Pier Luigi Nervi,** this ultramodern Catholic Cathedral cost $7 million. Its four arching white paraboloids converge to form the 200-foot-high concrete roof in the shape of a Greek cross. Inside, the prevalent feeling is one of vaulting space. A cross-shaped stained-glass window accents the ceiling, while four stained-glass windows rise from floor to ceiling in each main wall, representing the four elements. The cathedral seats 2,500 people around an impressive neo-primitive stone altar backed by a shiny wall of hanging aluminum rods.

The façade and interior of the St. Mary's Cathedral at the top of Cathedral Hill. The striking façade is made of Italian travertine.

Pier Luigi Nervi
(1891-1979)

This Italian engineer, trained in the great tradition of G. A. Eiffel, E. Freyssenet, and R. Maillart, won fame in Italy and worldwide as a designer of buildings in reinforced concrete buildings, a medium he skillfully exploited to attain the maximum technical and aesthetic profit. Nervi contributed significantly to the study of large-scale single-bay roofs. One very important example of this type of construction—besides St. Mary's Cathedral—is the Palazzo delle Esposizioni in Turin, Italy (1948). Also outstanding among Nervi's many works are the UNESCO building in Paris (1953-1957, with M. Breuer and B. Zehrfuss), the Papal Audience Chamber in Vatican City (1971), and the Pirelli Tower in Milan, Italy (1955-60, with G. Ponti).

Pietro Belluschi
(1899-1994)

The architect Pietro Belluschi, of Italian origin, came to the United States in 1923 and worked extensively all over the country.
The best-known and most exemplary of his works is of course New York's Pan Am building, in International Style, with its octagonal floor plan and facade in granite, glass, and cement. He designed this skyscraper, now the MetLife Building, in collaboration with Walter Gropius in 1962.

MUSEUMS

SAN FRANCISCO MUSEUM OF MODERN ART

The new quarters of the San Francisco Museum of Modern Art immediately became the city's greatest monument to city contemporary architecture when they were inaugurated in 1995. The resplendent new building, designed by the Swiss architect **Mario Botta**, certainly reasserted SF MOMA's standing among the world's major museums of contemporary art, but it is also a jewel in the Yerba Buena Gardens renewal project. The Modernist style of the building expresses both power and vision, or, in the words of its creator,

"Perfect equilibrium, where art and architecture mutually enrich each other." The five-story structure is clad in burnt-sienna brick and features a 125-foot-tall, black-and-white-striped cylinder cut at a dramatic angle and capped by a brilliant skylight. The center of the façade is marked by a vertical slot that gives the building an intriguing look. The ground floor entrance presents a broad glazed wall. Inside, the sun-filled atrium astounds, rising five floors to the skylight. A grand staircase leads from the atrium to the four floors of spacious galleries. The San Francisco Museum of Art opened in 1935; it didn't become the Museum of Modern Art until forty years later, when it was directed by Harry Hopkins. Today its modern 25,000 square foot new building is

home to over 20,000 pieces of art in many different mediums. The second floor is host to a collection of paintings and sculptures representing all the major schools and artists from the early 20th century through today. The museum is famous for its collections of Fauvist, Abstract Expressionist, Surrealist, Mexican Modernist, Bay Area Figurative, and Punk art. The galleries are thus showcases for the works of **Henri Matisse, Pablo Picasso, Frida Kahlo, William de Kooning, René Magritte, Ellsworth Kelly, Robert Rauschenberg, Mark Rothko, Andy Warhol**—and a myriad of others.

SF MOMA houses some of the world's greatest modern paintings.

Top left, Jeune fille aux yeux verts *(1908) and bottom left,* Femme au chapeau *(1905), both by Henri Matisse.*

Top right, Frida and Diego Rivera *(1931), by Frida Kahlo.*

Bottom right, Noel in the kitchen, *by Joan Brown.*

But there's more up there: the Architecture and Design section, inaugurated in 1983, a collection of sketches, plans, and objects by the most influential modern-day architects—**Frank O. Gehry, Frank Lloyd Wright, Charles** and **Ray Eames, Fumihiko Maki**—and many works of graphic art, like the more than 400 rock concert posters from the 1960's and 70's.

The third floor is the milieu for temporary exhibits and the museum's notable collection of photographs.

SF MOMA, top: Country Dog Gentlemen *(1972) by Roy de Forest.*
Center: Les valeurs personnels *(1952) by René Magritte.*
Black Place I *(1944) by Georgia O' Keeffe.*
Bottom: Berkeley # 23 *(1955) by Richard Diebenkorn.*

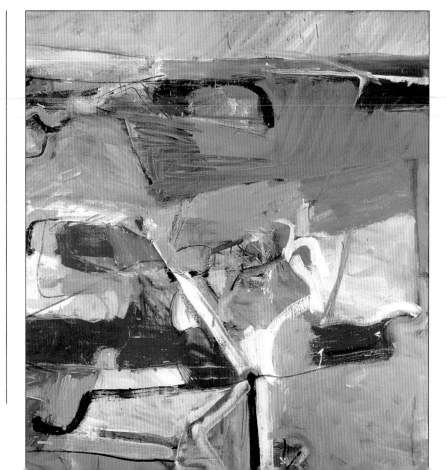

The SF MOMA was one of the first museums to recognize the artistic worth of this medium, and its showpieces include works by **Ansel Adams, Imogen Cunnigham, Alfred Stieglitz, Walker Evans,** and **Cindy Sherman**. Besides the great names, the museum also collects "vernacular photographs"– that is, photos by amateurs and documentary material originally produced with no artistic intent. On the fourth and last floor you'll find the museum's newest section: the Media Arts, which have come to maturity in San Francisco and the Bay Area over the last forty years. Here you'll find the video installations of such pioneers as **Bill Viola** and **Nam-Jun Paik** and the latest works by the director **Matthew Barney**.

Each year, the roomy premises of the SF MOMA accept about twenty temporary exhibits, which make a hefty contribution to upholding the reputation the city has won for itself over the years as a center for art and a supporter of all its forms of expression.

SF MOMA, top to bottom:
Ocean Park No. 54 *(1972) by Richard* Diebenkorn; Michael Jackson and Bubbles *(1988) by Jeff Koons;* The Mouse's Tale *(1951-54) by Jess;* California Artist *(1982) by Robert* Arneson.

Center: Geomechanical Tower; Inner Central Shaft, *from* Two Centricity *(1987), by Lebbeus Woods;* A to Z 1995 Travel Trailer Unit Customized *(1995), by Andrea Zittel and Charlie White.*

Top: In Joshua Tree National Monument, *California (1942) by Ansel Adams;* Untitled (Composizione il Duomo) *(Firenze, agosto 1983) by Aldo Rossi.*

Bottom: Model for Stitch Plan, Cleveland, Ohio Project *(1989) by Steven Holl.*
Right: La Négresse Blonde *(1933) by Constantin Brancusi.*

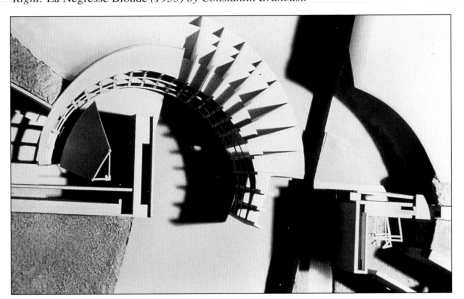

CALIFORNIA PALACE OF THE LEGION OF HONOR

From its hilltop perch in the Presidio, the Legion of Honor holds a commanding view of the city and the Golden gate Bridge spanning the bay. However stunning, the view is no more impressive than the building itself, a French-style palace designed by George Applegarth in 1916. Using the Palais de la Légion d'Honneur in Paris as a model, Applegarth designed the building with grand colonnades and a very triumphal arch.

The building was donated by Mr. and Mrs. Adolph Spreckels in 1924 to commemorate Californian soldiers lost in World War I.

The Palace of the Legion of Honor was completely renovated and reopened in 1995.

Outside, the museum has several notable statues, including two Rodin masterpieces, *The Thinker* and *The Shades*, which foreshadow the delights of the Rodin Gallery inside, where over seventy of his works are displayed.

The museum was devoted exclusively to French art until the early 1990s, when the M.H. de Young Museum donated a vast European collection.

The museum's present holdings span eight centuries through the early twentieth century and include paintings, sculptures and decorative arts. Among the early masters whose works hang here are Rubens, Rembrandt, Van Dyck and El Greco; later masters include Degas, Cézanne, Seurat, Renoir, Manet and Monet. Period rooms beautifully capture long-lost times and places.

Below and on the facing page, top, classical and modern elements typify the exteriors of the restored Palace of the Legion of Honor.

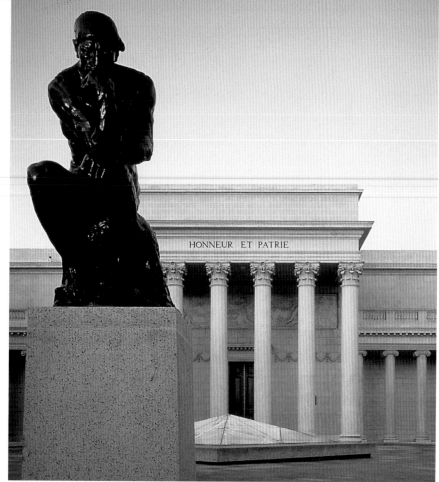

Downstairs the museum holds the largest collection of graphic prints in the West. All told, in both presentation and content, the Legion of Honor is splendid.

The Palace of the Legion of Honor, completely renovated and reopened in 1995, is home to the **Fine Arts Museums of San Francisco.**

The Thinker (1904) by Auguste Rodin, in the Court of Honor.

The Bath *(1880-85) by Jean-Léon Gérôme;*
Flowers in a Vase *(1882) by Henri Fantin-Latour.*

Portrait of Joris de Caulerij *(1632) by Rembrandt.*

The Russian Bride's Attire *(1889) by Konstantin
Makovsky.*

Still Life with Skull, Leeks, and Pitcher
(1945) by Pablo Picasso.

*Japanned bureau cabinet,
English, c. 1730, Japanned
wood, 92 1/2" x 47 1/2 x
27", no artist
recorded.*

Kneeling Youth
*(*Adolescent à
genoux*) (ca. 1925)
by Georges Minne.*

M.H. DE YOUNG MEMORIAL MUSEUM

Two Women and a Child *(1926), by Diego Rivera.*

The idea for the museum was conceived by *San Francisco Chronicle* publisher Michael de Young, who organized the California Midwinter International Exposition of 1894 on 200 acres in the park. De Young promoted the fair far and wide and used the proceeds to fund a permanent art museum for the city. The museum's galleries hold the city's main collection of American art, which includes paintings, sculptures and decorative arts from Colonial times to the twentieth century. Some of the American masters on display are William Harnett, John Peto, Alexander Pope, John Singleton Copley, James Peale, Mary Cassatt, John Singer Sargent and James McNeill Whistler.
Modern American greats include the works of Wayne Thiebaud, Georgia O'Keeffe, Grant Wood and Reginald Marsh.
A brand new De Young Memorial Museum is planned to be built on the same site as the original building (1919), and it will be ready by the year 2005.

Oranges in Tissue Paper *(ca. 1890) by William J. McCloskey.*

M. H. de Young Memorial Museum:

Top, left, Caroline de Bassano, Marquise d'Espeuilles *(1884) by John Singer Sargent.*

Top right, The Bright Side *(1865) by Winslow Homer.*

Right, Job Lot Cheap *(1892) by John Frederick Peto.*

Below, The Ironworkers' Noontime *(1880) by Thomas Pollock Anshutz, 1880.*

PALACE OF FINE ARTS

Designed by architect Bernard Maybeck as the centerpiece of the Panama-Pacific International Exposition of 1915, the Palace of Fine Arts was such a huge success that it was left standing after the Exposition ended. For years the Palace slowly decayed until a city benefactor donated funds to restore it in 1962.

The restoration was completed in 1969, the year the **Exploratorium Science Museum** was opened inside the Palace. The Exposition of 1915 marked the opening of the Panama Canal, but more significantly celebrated the rebirth of the city reduced to rubble and ash in 1906. For that reason Maybeck's triumphal design struck a chord in the hearts of San Franciscans. Set in a lovely park with a duck pond, Maybeck's classical Roman rotunda looms majestically over two Corinthian colonnades. A top the colonnades are beautifully sculpted weeping maidens and a remarkable entablature cast in high relief.

The Palace of Fine Arts and the Exploratorium Science Museum.

Opposite, Exploratorium Science Museum: Kaleidoscope, Distorted Room, Shadow Wal, Gift Store.

THE EXPLORATORIUM SCIENCE MUSEUM

*O*ne of the finest children's science museums in the country, the Exploratorium Science Museum was founded by Frank Oppenheimer—whose brother Robert invented the atomic bomb—on the premise that one learns by doing. The 650 hands-on exhibits, therefore, all require some degree of visitor participation to reveal the physical wonders of the world. The **Tactile Dome** within the museum creates an intriguing, vacuous environment void of most physical sensations.

WELLS FARGO BANK HISTORY MUSEUM

Inspired by Gold Rush fever, upstate New Yorkers Henry Wells and William George Fargo met with their associates in New York City to create a joint stock company in March of 1852. The company was to act as a commercial liaison between New York City and San Francisco, conducting banking and other business ventures between the two coastal cities and all points in between. In July of 1852, Wells, Fargo & Company opened shop on San Francisco's Montgomery Street, not ten feet from where the Wells Fargo Bank History Museum stands today. Only three years later, Wells Fargo was a financial powerhouse, with fifty-five offices nationwide; by 1890, there were 2,600 Wells Fargo branches across the country. The Museum, then, is well-deserved and provides a fascinating historical perspective of the meteoric rise of a fledgling business venture and—at the same time—San Francisco itself. The Museum is connected to the bank's central office, located around the corner on California Street. The 4,400-square-foot Museum exhibits artifacts from the Gold Rush and the dawn of transcontinental travel: mining equipment, gold nuggets, period photographs and early banking paraphernalia are on display. The crowd favorite is the authentic nineteenth-century, red-and-yellow-painted stagecoach made in Concord, New Hampshire. Upstairs, visitors can sit in a reproduction stagecoach while listening to a narration describing the travails of the interminable voyage from the East. Also upstairs is a display commemorating Charles E. Bolton, alias Black Bart, who robbed twenty-eight stagecoaches in the 1870s and 80s.

Besides mastering the art of highway robbery, Black Bart was famous for the notes of poetry he left at the scene of his crimes. Amazingly, Black Bart was apprehended after carelessly dropping a handkerchief that was traced to a laundry on Bush Street. Black Bart served only four years at San Quentin State Penitentiary, after which he was paroled for good behavior. He was never heard from again.

Wells Fargo Bank History Museum: a well-rigged Stagecoach.

ASIAN ART MUSEUM

The Asian Art Museum was opened in 1966 after Avery Brundage donated his renowned Asian art collection to the city. An engineering mogul known better as the long-serving president of the International Olympic Committee, Brundage amassed his collection over a lifetime. He chose to donate it to San Francisco because of the city's long-standing social links with Asia. Today the collection totals more than 12,000 pieces, making the museum the largest of its kind in the U.S. Artworks range from paintings and sculptures to all imaginable decorative arts. The exhibit includes works from Korea and China, the focus of Brundage's passionate collecting, as well as from the rest of Asia. Housed for several years in the de Young Museum's west wing, the Museum is planned to be moved to its new Civic Center home in 2003.

SAN FRANCISCO ART INSTITUTE

Founded in 1871, the San Francisco Art Institute is the oldest art school on the West Coast and remains one of the top art training centers in the country. The impressive building, a Spanish Colonial-style "monastery" with a medieval concrete tower and a serene interior courtyard surrounded by an architrave, was built in 1926 by San Francisco architects Bakewell & Brown after the institute moved from its perch on Nob Hill.

The institute's **Diego Rivera Gallery** should not be missed. Rivera briefly taught at the institute in the early 1930s, and his large mural in the gallery honors the American Worker.

William Lewis Gerstle sponsored the mural, and his personage is portrayed in the man wearing the black hat.

The facade of the San Francisco Art Institute.

CALIFORNIA ACADEMY OF SCIENCES

The West's oldest scientific institution, the California Academy of Sciences was founded on Market Street in 1853. After the original Academy was destroyed by fire in 1906, it opened its doors in the park in 1916. The Academy's grandiose building faces the M.H. de Young Museum and includes museums, exhibition halls, a planetarium and an aquarium. The Academy's Natural History Museum includes a remarkable Gem and Mineral Hall as well as the Hohfeld Earth and Space Hall, which has an exhibit that simulates the tremors of the city's two famous quakes. The Wild California and African Safari galleries show the diversity of both habitat's wildlife. The Discovery Room for Children presents many interesting hands-on exhibitions that aren't just for kids. Under a sixty-five-foot-high dome, the Morrison Planetarium is northern California's largest indoor solar system. The dome serves as backdrop for highly entertaining sky shows. The Planetarium's Laserium features a choreographed, one-hour laser show accompanied by throbbing rock music. Perhaps the most impressive section in the Academy, the Steinhart Aquarium displays the world's most diverse collection of sea creatures, including over 14,000 species of fish. There is also a simulated swamp that features a host of creepy reptiles and amphibians such as alligators, lizards and turtles. Another exhibit has dolphins, seals and penguins playing to the crowd. The most spectacular display, however, is the 100,000-gallon Fish Roundabout, a glass-enclosed tunnel surrounded on all sides by thousands of fish, including sharks and sting rays.

The facade of the California Academy of Sciences in Golden Gate Park.

The building of the San Francisco National Maritime Museum.

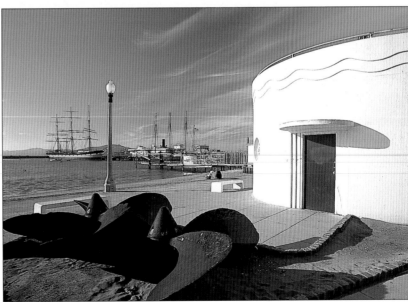

The distinctive building that since 1951 is home to the SF National Maritime Museum, with tall ships in the background.

SAN FRANCISCO NATIONAL MARITIME MUSEUM

The National Maritime Museum captures the essence of San Francisco from its beginnings as a small frontier seaport. Since those early days, the small town has became a major metropolis, but an affinity for the sea has remained. The Maritime Museum chronicles the city's seafaring history with countless photographs, nautical instruments and model ship displays. The building itself is remarkable for its ship-shaped, art deco façade that still maintains many of its original 1930s features. Moored nearby at the Hyde Street Pier is one of the world's largest collections of old ships, including such tall beauties as the *CA Thayer* and the *Balclutha*.

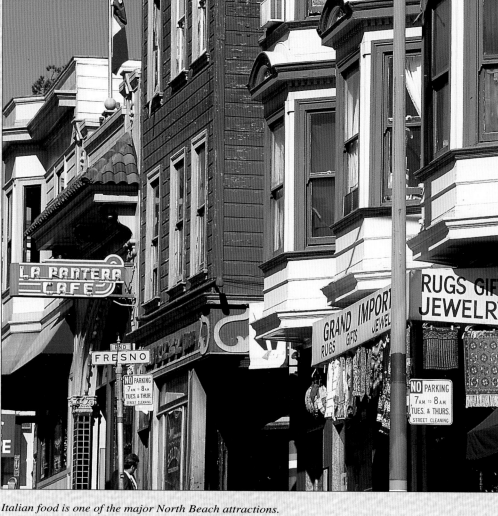

Italian food is one of the major North Beach attractions.

NORTH BEACH

*T*he beach that stretched between Telegraph and Russian Hills disappeared under landfill long ago, but North Beach remains one of the most exciting areas in the city. In many ways North Beach represents a lifestyle. On one hand it is known as "Little Italy" and is the historic center of the Italian community. On the other hand, North Beach is the traditional home of young bohemians and other radical intellectuals, the social fringe made famous by the Beatnik (a term coined by Herb Caen) generation of the 1950s. Conveniently, these two mythic forces— the Mediterranean and the angst-ridden—blend quite amicably in North Beach's exuberant cafe-oriented atmosphere.

Although North Beach is still intimately known as Little Italy, in fact the Italians were not the first nor the last to arrive here. Chilean prostitutes came first, lured by the Gold Rush in the 1850s. Then came the Irish, and finally the Italians after the turn of the century. By 1940, Italians were the largest foreign-born population in the city. The Chinese, however, were soon to arrive to North Beach. While Broadway was once considered the boundary between North Beach and Chinatown, during the 1960s the Chinese began crossing the border and settling in Little Italy. Today the population is more than fifty percent Chinese. Nevertheless, the Italian culture is a resilient one, and the neighborhood has retained its ethnic flavor. The annual Columbus Day Parade in October is still the biggest celebration of the year, and Italians still stream to the North Beach playground to play bocce. Most importantly, Italian cuisine still reigns supreme. North Beach remains the home of some of the city's best Italian restaurants, bakeries and cafes.

"Vesuvio" became one of North Beach's most famous bars during the Beat era.

Broadway at night in the adult entertainement district.

AROUND COLUMBUS AVENUE

Columbus Avenue cuts a wide diagonal swath through North Beach and is home to several San Francisco institutions. **City Lights Bookstore** is the city's famous literary institution. Opened by Beatnik poet Lawrence Ferlinghetti, City Lights grabbed the spotlight in 1956 with the publication of Allen Ginsberg's controversial poem *Howl*, which was widely condemned as obscene and pornographic. Across Jack Kerouac Street is **Vesuvio Cafe**, serving bohemians the likes of Dylan Thomas since 1949. Across Columbus is **Tosca Cafe**, a great place to see and be seen while listening to the jukebox play opera's greatest hits. The four blocks of Columbus between Filbert and Broadway are the busiest in Little Italy and feature back-to-back restaurants and cafes and are quite a scene on weekends. Although tattoos and body piercings are not for everyone, the **Tattoo Art Museum** on Columbus Avenue certainly makes a strong case. This working tattoo parlor is lined with photographs of extravagant body decorations that make even the prudent pause and ponder. More of North Beach's cultural treasures are found along **Upper Grant Avenue**, just north of Broadway and the **Condor**

Club, where the modern world's first topless stage show was performed by Carol Doda in 1964. These blocks of restaurants, bars and coffee shops are some of the city's oldest and favorite places to spend a relaxing afternoon. A watering hole since 1861, **The Saloon** is one of these beloved city landmarks. At the corner of Vallejo, another is **Caffè Trieste**, the oldest coffeehouse in San Francisco and a popular hangout for Beatnik artists and writers in the 1950s. A time-honored tradition, Trieste offers live opera on Saturday afternoons. Just north is the **Lost and Found Saloon**, now a blues club but formerly the Coffee Gallery, another legendary Beatnik haunt. Built in 1912 as an Italian community hall, **Club Fugazi** has been home to "Beach Blanket Babylon", the city's most famous musical cabaret, for over two decades. Steve Silver's zany show is now a cultural institution, popular with locals and tourists alike. Although the themes change annually, each production is a bonfire of vanities, parodying the schmaltz of pop culture as well as that of the old city itself. The cabaret features a high-energy cast wearing outlandish costumes— especially bizarre, gigantic hats.

The signs of the Vesuvio Café, the City Lights Bookstore, and the Tosca Café are among the attractions in North Beach.

Jack Kerouac (1922-1969)

Although born in Lowell, Massachusetts, the writer Jack Kerouac was one of the most representative figures of the Beat Generation, the artistic movement spawned in San Francisco in the 1950's. His novel *On the Road* is even considered its manifesto. Kerouac's nearly equally famous *Dharma Bums* and *Big Sur* were inspired by life in the Bay Area in those years.

BEACH BLANKET BABYLON

Bust of Steve Silver in front of Club Fugazi, the permanent home of Beach Blanket Babylon.

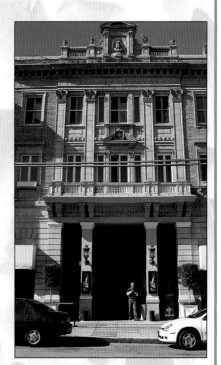

When it debuted in June of 1974, this irreverent parody of contemporary American culture, with its exaggeratedly extravagant costumes and unique, enormous headgear, was an immediate smash hit with the theater-going public. *Beach Blanket Babylon* is now one of the greatest successes in the history of musical comedy, having way back in 1984 topped the long-run record set by the legendary Ziegfeld Follies. In 1996 the street that hosts Club Fugazi, the permanent home of this show, was renamed Beach Blanket Babylon Boulevard. The BBB set sees a constant turnover as new characters, songs, and naturally costumes are added yearly in response to the flux of contemporary culture. The present version, for example, presents Ozzi Osbourne, Martha Stewart, Anne Nicole Smith, Hillary Clinton, Oprah and Brittney Spears.

Top, right, the elegant entrance to the Club Fugazi.

Scenes and characters from Beach Blanket Babylon.

91

WASHINGTON SQUARE

The centerpiece of North Beach, Washington Square also happens to be one of the finest urban parks in the United States. With its peripheral shield of trees and broad expanse of lawn, Washington Square fits in perfectly against its urban backdrop. Although the park is the lowest depression between Russian and Telegraph hills, the sense of open space is powerful and refreshing. The surrounding buildings are conveniently unimposing—low and light-colored—and seem only to enhance the park's bucolic setting. The Square, in fact, has a cozy, small town feeling, which couldn't be more appropriate for North Beach life.

Reserved as a park by Mayor Jasper O'Farrell in 1847, Washington Square's current landscape was designed in 1955. In the center of this simple park stands a statue of Benjamin Franklin, a gift of H.D. Cogswell in 1879. Cogswell happened to be an outspoken teetotaler, which was apparent in 1979 when the time-capsule under the monument was opened to reveal tomes of temperance tracts. (Incidentally, the time capsule was refilled with a bottle of wine, a pair of Levi's jeans and some verses by Beatnik poet Lawrence Ferlinghetti; it will be reopened in 2079.) The monument's water taps—now long dry—are inscribed in the spirit of prohibition: "Cal Seltzer," "Vichy" and "Congress."

On the Columbus Avenue side of the park is a sentimental bronze statue that honors the city's volunteer firemen. Donated by the eccentric Lillie Hitchcock Coit, who was rescued from a burning house as a child, the monument was erected in 1933. Fittingly enough, it depicts two firemen with a rescued child. The park is the meeting place for young and old, especially the Italian - and Chinese-American families that live in the neighborhood. There is a certain social order here: older men tend to sit on the benches along Union Street, while young people stretch out on the lawn and children frolic in the playground area. Just like in small towns everywhere.

Benjamin Franklin's statue stands in the center of Washington Square.

The Romanesque façade of Saints Peter and Paul Catholic Church.

SAINTS PETER AND PAUL ROMAN CATHOLIC CHURCH

A majestic crown to the north side of the park, Saints Peter and Paul Church was designed by Charles Fantoni. The Romanesque church, distinguished by its stately twin spires, took two decades to construct and was finally dedicated in 1924. Interestingly, as the Church was being built, famed Hollywood director Cecil B. DeMille filmed the construction to depict the building of the Temple of Jerusalem in his 1953 film *The Ten Commandments*.

Still known as the Italian Cathedral, Saints Peter and Paul is a symbol of the Italian community even today, when the original Italian core has long dispersed and area is predominantly Chinese.

The Church has been so central to the Italian community, in fact, that it has also been known as "Fishermen's Church" because so many Italians in the community once earned their living by fishing. A mass celebrating the Blessing of the Fleet is still held every October, when a procession migrates from the Church to Fisherman's Wharf. A testament to the Church's importance within the Italian community, local baseball hero Joe Di Maggio was photographed here after his marriage to Marilyn Monroe in 1957.

The building was constructed with a steel frame covered with white concrete. The interior is quite complex, notable for its many columns and ornate, extravagant altar, which depicts a beatific city adorned with a horizon of marble spires and life-size angels. The Church is filled with statues, mosaics and beautiful stained-glass windows.

CHINATOWN

The largest Chinese community on the West Coast, San Francisco's Chinatown is home to many of the Bay Area's 120,000 Chinese-Americans. In the U.S., only New York City's Chinatown is larger. Unlike New York's settlement, however, San Francisco's Chinatown is an integrated focus of city life.

The streets of Chinatown are noisy and garish and jam-packed with people. The atmosphere is quite hectic. One of the main draws here is cheap, delicious food: there are countless restaurants in Chinatown as well as numerous shops loaded with fresh fish and Chinese vegetables. On the weekends, it's a great place to go for dim sum, the traditional Chinese a la carte brunch, followed by a not-very-leisurely—but highly entertaining—stroll among the Chinese bric-a-brac shops, especially along **Grant Avenue**. Lined with dragon lamp-posts and buildings with fancy, turned-up tile roofs, Grant is the major tourist attraction in Chinatown. The streets here are raucous all day and late into the night. To really enjoy Chinatown, however,

one must get off the beaten track and explore. Then you might discover the culinary pleasures of **Stockton Street**, where locals do their shopping. Here one finds some of the freshest vegetables, produce and fish in the city. Around the corner on Ross Alley, the **Golden Gate Fortune Cookie Company** allows customers to taste samples of their prophetic cookies—a local invention—which of course are now eaten around the world.

Although only two blocks long, **Waverly Place** is perhaps Chinatown's most intriguing find. During the Tong Wars of the late nineteenth century, Waverly Place was one of the scariest areas in the city.

The streets were lined with brothels until the disaster of 1906, after which several Chinese community associations and two important temples were built. Today Waverly is known as "the street of painted balconies," for obvious reasons.

Chinatown: a shopping street lined with dragon lamps.

A cable car adds a note of color to the streets of Chinatown.

Chinatown Market, night view.

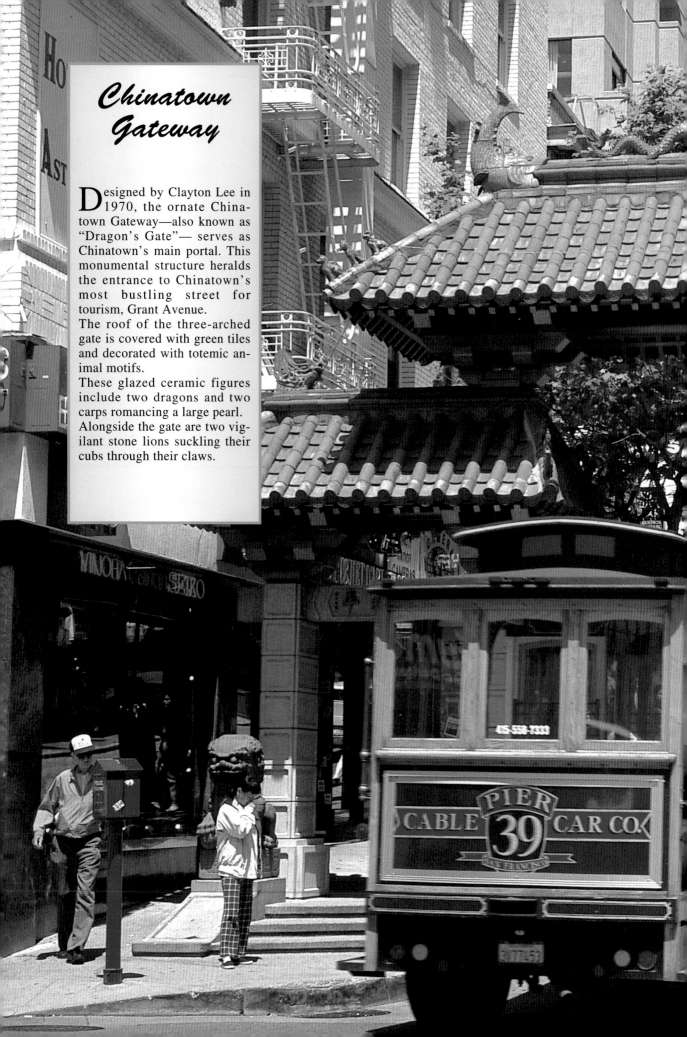

Chinatown Gateway

Designed by Clayton Lee in 1970, the ornate Chinatown Gateway—also known as "Dragon's Gate"— serves as Chinatown's main portal. This monumental structure heralds the entrance to Chinatown's most bustling street for tourism, Grant Avenue.

The roof of the three-arched gate is covered with green tiles and decorated with totemic animal motifs.

These glazed ceramic figures include two dragons and two carps romancing a large pearl. Alongside the gate are two vigilant stone lions suckling their cubs through their claws.

San Francisco's
famous
Chinatown,
the largest outside
of China itself.

PORTSMOUTH SQUARE

With so much to see and do in San Francisco, it is easy to forget that Portsmouth Square was the birthplace of the city, once part of Mexican territory. In 1839 the Mexican government called on Swiss engineer Jean Jacques Vioget to plot out the town of what was then known as Yerba Buena, a mere cluster of adobe huts along Grant Avenue and simple frame buildings along the shore. The area Vioget plotted, with its short, narrow blocks and tiny lots, is still preserved in Chinatown. Portsmouth Square was the town's main plaza.

The square got its present name in 1846, when war broke out between Mexico and the United States. The *U.S.S. Portsmouth* swiftly took over the port town. In 1848, the Mexican peace treaty officially ceded the entire Southwest to the United States.

One year later, on May 12, 1849, Samuel Brennan, editor of the *California Star*, stood in Portsmouth Square and announced the discovery of gold in the foothills of the Sierra Nevada. Thus the California Gold Rush began, and San Francisco would soon become a major metropolis.

Portsmouth Square remained the hub of the growing city for the next decade or so, but in the 1860s business interests would shift to the landfill along the Bay in the southeast. Slowly the plaza declined in civic importance, although even today the square remains a busy and densely packed thoroughfare, a playground of sorts for Chinatown residents to commune, play cards and, in the morning, practice *t'ai chi*.

When Robert Louis Stevenson lived in San Francisco in the late 1870s, he would sit in the square and absorb the sights and sounds of the bustling city. The

Hispaniola Monument stands in the northwest corner of the square commemorating him. The **Goddess of Democracy** also rests here, a monument to the 1989 Tiananmen Square protests in Beijing. In the Holiday Inn across the footbridge from the square, the **Chinese Culture Center** features exhibitions of Chinese-American artists and writers.

TIEN HAU TEMPLE

Set among the painted balconies of Waverly Place, Tien Hau Temple occupies the top floor of a yellow-brick building designed in 1911 by the ubiquitous O'Brien Brothers. Dedicated to Tien Hau, Queen of Heaven and protector of seafarers and visitors, the Temple was founded in 1852 and is the oldest Chinese place of worship in the country.
At the top of three steep, wooden flights of stairs, the Temple opens onto another world entirely. The ceiling is covered with hundreds of gold and red lanterns, and the air is heavy with the scent of incense and burnt paper offerings. Red electric bulbs and oil candles light this narrow space, which is furnished with antiques from other temples destroyed when the Chinese were driven from remote California towns in the 1880s. Gift oranges lie on the carved altar, behind which a wooden statue of Tien Hau watches rather ominously.

BANK OF CANTON

The most authentically Chinese building in all of Chinatown, the Bank of Canton is a wonderful spectacle to behold. Built in 1909, the three-tiered tower was home to the Chinatown Telephone Exchange until the 1950s, when the Bank of Canton acquired it. The building is an impressive work of architectural chinoiserie that has been well preserved by the Bank. It appears much like a pagoda, with the three upward-curving, ceramic-tiled rooves accenting the red walls and intricate, geometric tracery windows.
Originally, the telephone operators were all male and had to be fluent in English as well as five different Chinese dialects. They worked on the main floor and had sleeping quarters on the second. Since there is no Chinese alphabet, the telephone directory was arranged by street. A copy of an early telephone book—handwritten—is on display at the Chinese Historical Society.

The Tien Hau Temple is the oldest Chinese place of worship in the United States. Tien Hau is the goddess of navigators and visitors.

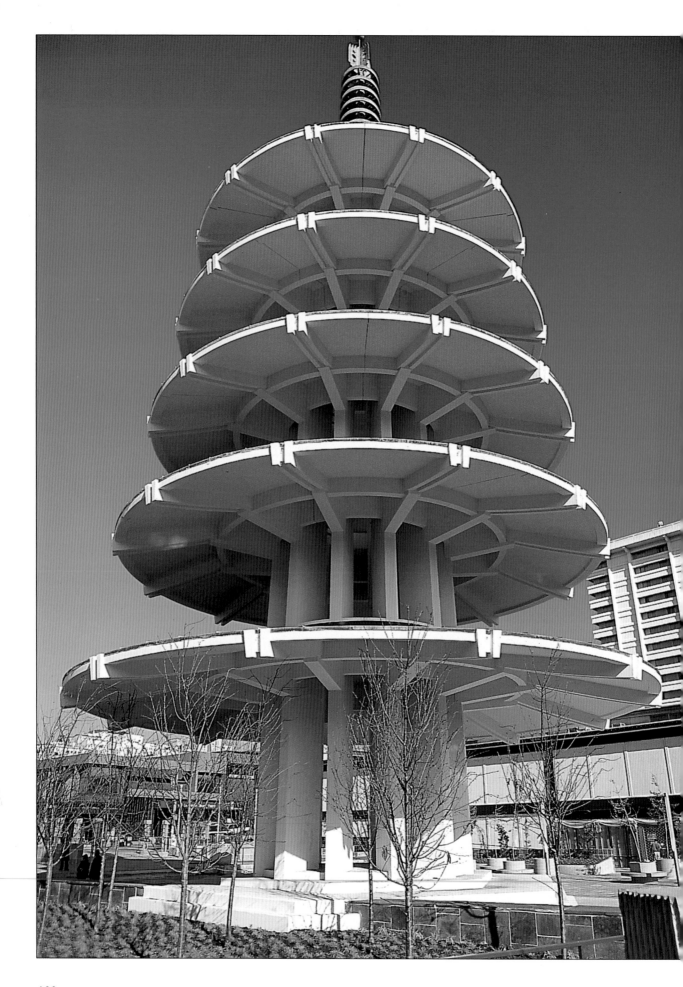

JAPANTOWN

The majority of Japantown's Japanese population lost their homes during the internment of World War II.

Although only four percent of the city's Japanese now live within Japantown's twenty square blocks, the area retains its cultural flavor and many of its ethnic traditions. On weekends the streets of Nihonmachi, as Japantown is called locally, are the site of many age-old rituals and festivals. Many of the properties are decorated with stone lanterns and impressive topiary bushes. The block-long **Buchanan Mall** is landscaped like a traditional Japanese flower garden with fountains designed by renowned sculptor Ruth Asawa.

BUDDHIST CHURCH OF SAN FRANCISCO

The Buddhist Church of San Francisco was built by *nisei* architect Gentoko Shimamato in 1938, only a few years before the local Japanese population would be interned in the Utah desert during World War II. During the internment years, the church was maintained by its converted non-Japanese members. The façade of the church is a Roman Baroque design with broken pediments and a dome and finial, which are said to house the relics of the Buddha donated by the King of Siam in 1935. Contrary to its façade, the inside of the church is one of the most peaceful sanctuaries in the city. Up a broad staircase on the second floor, the worship hall is serene and transcendent. The gilded altar is surrounded by beautiful painted screens of peacocks, while the simple wall beams are adorned with ornate gilded panels carved in Kyoto.

PEACE PAGODA

The centerpiece of Japan Center, the five-acre shopping and entertainment complex built in 1968, the Peace Pagoda is a 100-foot-tall, five-tiered concrete monument to civic harmony. Rising from the center of Peace Plaza, the pagoda was designed by architect Yoshiro Taniguchi of Tokyo. Although Taniguchi is a respected authority on ancient Japanese architecture, his pagoda looks very modern, like a futuristic radio antenna. Surrounding the plaza are the shopping center's many malls, filled with Japanese shops and restaurants.

The Peace Pagoda of Japan Center and the unmistakable style of the buildings in Japantown.

THE HAIGHT

*T*he Haight district comprises several diverse social communities, including those of Golden Gate Park, Buena Vista Hill and the legendary Haight-Ashbury neighborhood. The physical landscape is as variegated as the population, as grand mansions often rub shoulders with run-down townhouses. Developed later than the other neighborhoods on the fringe of the city, the Haight was lucky to rise in the Victorian splendor of the 1890s. The **Panhandle**, the narrow, eight-block stretch of park along Oak Street, was intended as a carriage entry to Golden Gate Park. Like the rest of the neighborhood, it was lined with stately Victorian homes, many of which still stand today with brand new coats of paint.

The neighborhood's decline began in 1917, however, when construction of the Twin Peaks tunnel lured denizens of the Haight out to the more secluded and spacious city limits. This trend of decay persisted through the 1950s. In the 1960s, low rents and good karma attracted infamous hordes of hippies to the neighborhood, which became the mecca of the entire Love Generation. The decline of the Haight continued. Only in the past decade has the Haight been reborn, undergoing vast gentrification. Today the Haight is home to many young, middle- and upper-class professionals.

A sign in Haight Street.

SUMMER OF LOVE

*I*n 1967, the Summer of Love transformed the dilapidated neighborhood known as Haight-Ashbury. 200,000 young people pilgrimaged to **Haight-Ashbury** that summer, lured by the promise of peace, love and understanding. Those brief three months would define an entire generation as well as the neighborhood where that generation was born. Secluded by surrounding parkland and mired in glorious decay, Haight-Ashbury was a perfect place to launch the hippie revolution. Kids came to act against the Establishment and to indulge their wildest dreams of communal living, drugs, sex and music. This small community nurtured some of the most legendary rock musicians of all time: the Grateful Dead rested their heads at **710 Ashbury Street**; Janis Joplin resided at **122 Lyon Street**; Jefferson Airplane took off from **2400 Fulton Street**. When the party was finally over in the 1970s and the last guests had trickled out, Haight-Ashbury had a lot of cleaning up to do. Now the neighborhood is on the rise again, the home to a solidly established professional class.

Left, fans paying tribute to the memory of Jerry Garcia (1942-1995); right, the Haight Street Fair.

THE CASTRO

*T*he Castro proudly boasts the city's largest gay population. Perhaps nowhere else in the world do gay men wield such political might and enjoy such broad social acceptance. Castro Street is the main thoroughfare, lined with restaurants, bars, cafes, stores and boutiques that openly cater to the gay community. The neighborhood's biggest celebrations are the Gay Freedom Day parade in June and the Halloween extravaganza, which brings out all the ghouls and goblins on October 31. The Castro is a stylish and well-maintained neighborhood that does a good job assimilating modern architecture into the Victorian landscape.

Market Street links the inner Castro district with the San Francisco Bay waterfront.

Victorian homes in The Castro.

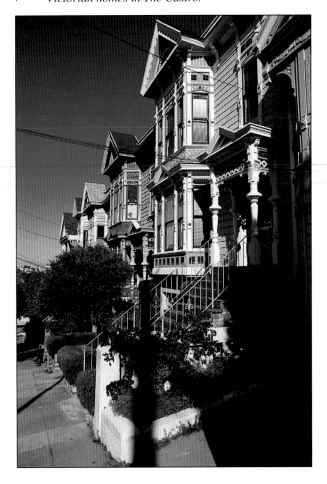

NOE VALLEY

*N*oe Valley is a self-sufficient community, quite indifferent to the goings-on downtown. At the border of the Mission District and the Haight Ashbury, Noe Valley is a comfy neighborhood and a pleasant place to stroll around without being in a touristy area. It's an engaging mixture of eclectic shops and coffeehouses. The area was named after José de Jesus Noe, the last Mexican mayor of the city then known as Yerba Buena. Today there is a bohemian element, once compared to New York's Greenwich Village, as well as a young, professional contingent that arrived in the 1970s, when downtown real estate became unaffordable. 24th Street has all the commercial interests any small city could offer, and the Victorian homes are homey and well-kept. The neighborhood has a remarkable small-town feel.

THE MISSION

A sheltered valley on the fringe of San Francisco, The Mission District was one of the earliest settlements in the Bay Area. When the focus of the city switched to Yerba Buena Cove in the early 1850s, The Mission became something of a suburb. Although settled first by the local Ohlone tribe and then Spanish missionaries, by the end of the nineteenth century it was inhabited largely by Irish immigrants. The area survived the calamities of 1906 in good form, and to this day some of the city's oldest and finest Victorian homes can be found here.

Today The Mission is once again largely Hispanic and still feels rather suburban. The streets are wide and the buildings low and—guarded by the hills from the fog rolling in off the Bay—The Mission enjoys the city's finest weather. Cinco de Mayo, which commemorates the victory of Mexican troops over Napolean III's invasion forces in 1862, is the area's most festive celebration. Because rents are generally cheap, The Mission has a strong bohemian culture as well.

Along **24th Street** from Mission to Bryant is the heart of the Latino shopping and restaurant district. The Mission has one of the West Coast's most complex Latino communities, and 24th Street caters largely to them. As a result of various civil wars in Central and South America, many Latino immigrants have settled in The Mission and opened up shop. There are Spanish-speaking Nicaraguan, Costa Rican and Salvadoran restaurants and specialty stores. Markets provide exotic tropical fruits and vegetables. The ambience is very much Latino in flavor.

A panoramic view of the Mission District, dominated by Dolores Park in the foreground.

The Fire Hydrant that Saved San Francisco

Why is this humble fire hydrant at the corner of 20th and Church Streets—near Dolores Park—known as the savior of San Francisco? When the 1906 earthquake shattered the city's water system it decommissioned the great majority of the fire-fighting hydrants. This one in the Mission District was one of the few that remained operational during San Francisco's Great Fire, and what's more it was its water that finally brought the flames under control. Every year, on the anniversary of the 1906 earthquake, the survivors gather to give it another coat of gold paint. For more information about the history of fires and fire-fighters in San Francisco, visit the San Francisco Fire Department Museum at 655 Presidio Avenue.

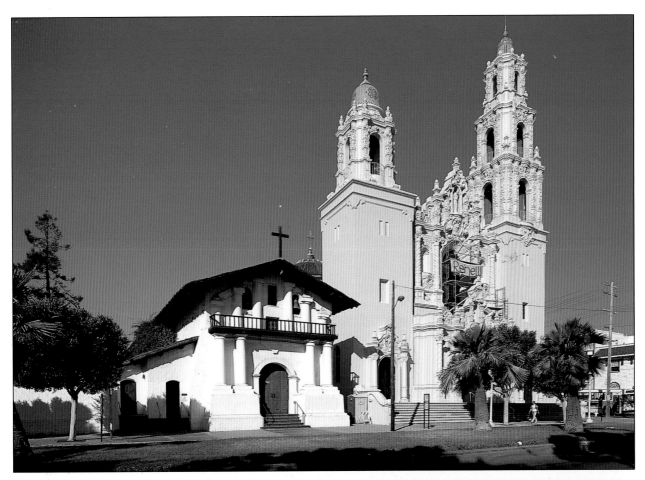

Mission Dolores. Top to bottom, the front of the 1791 mission building alongside the Basilica, a view of the interior, and, bottom, the interior of the Basilica.

MISSION DOLORES

San Francisco's first mission, Mission Dolores was settled by Spanish clerics led by Captain José Moraga in 1776. The current building was built in 1791, which makes the mission the oldest standing building in the city. Although the mission was originally dedicated to St. Francis of Assisi, it later assumed patronage by Our Lady of Sorrows. Mission Dolores was the sixth of the twenty-one missions founded by Mexicans along El Camino Real, the historic road leading all the way from Mexico to Sonoma, California. The crusade of missionaries was directed by Father Serra, who was beatified by the Roman Catholic Church in 1988. The mission's four-foot adobe walls have survived four major earthquakes. It is the only one of the original missions that is still standing and has not needed extensive repair. The painted ceilings were patterned after Ohlone tribal basket designs, and all the decorations, including the statues, altars and bells, were carried from Mexico along El Camino Real by packs of mules. Behind the mission is a picturesque old cemetery with the remains of some of the city's earliest pioneers and settlers. Included are over 5,000 members of the Ohlone tribe who were wiped out by measles in the early 1800s.

Opposite: "Keep Our Ancient Roots Alive" © 1995 Susan Kelk Cervantes, on Cleveland Elementary School, Persia & Athens Streets.

Top and right: "Family Life & The Spirit of Mankind" © 1977 Susan Kelk Cervantes & Judith Jamerson, on Flynn Elementary School, at Harrison & Precita Streets.

THE MISSION DISTRICT MURALS

The many brightly colored murals that make a walk through the Mission District a unique experience are the direct heirs of the age-old art of fresco painting. In 20th century San Francisco, these paintings on the facades and indeed any outside wall of buildings became a form of artistic expression typical of the city's Latino community, and in fact the majority of San Francisco's about 600 murals have been painted since the 1970's in the Mission District neighborhood. More information on the history and technique of murals can be found at the Precita Eyes Mural Arts and Visitors Center which also organizes guided tours.

Precita Eyes Mural Arts and Visitor Center, 2981 24th Street, Phone (415) 285 2287, www.precitaeyes.org.

"Carnaval" © *1996 Josh Sarantitis, Emmanuel Montoya, and Precita Eyes Muralists,*
at Harrison and 19th Street.

Page 110: "Silent Language of the Soul/ El Lenguaje Mudo del Alma" © 1990 Susan Kelk Cervantes & Juana Alicia. On Cesar Chavez Elementary School, on Shotwell between 22nd & 23nd Streets.

The mural "Golden Dream of the New World", by Daniel Galvez, 1984, at 24th Street and South Van Ness.

Levi Strauss & Co.

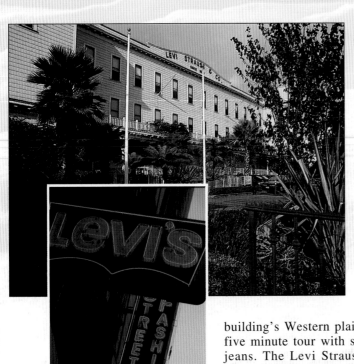

"[...] blue jeans: the most spectacular, the most practical, the most relaxed and nonchalant. They have expression, modesty, sex appeal, simplicity" (Yves Saint Laurent)

One of the basic items in any contemporary wardrobe, a cultural symbol and an unparalleled success in the history of fashion, blue jeans, were invented in San Francisco. In 1853 a Bavarian immigrant named Levi Strauss and his partner the tailor Jacob Davis patented a unique type of work pants and began amassing an immense fortune. Since the 1906 earthquake, the Levi Strauss & Co. factory has been located at 250 Valencia Street.

In 1970 the factory was given a face-lift by Howard Friedman, who designed the building's Western plains, cowboy look. The factory offers a forty-five minute tour with short film that chronicles the history of Levi jeans. The Levi Strauss Playground in front of the building was donated to the city by philanthropist Rosalie Stern.

The old headquarters and the trade-mark of Levi Strauss & Company.

TELEGRAPH HILL

Telegraph Hill is another of San Francisco's quaint and prestigious residential districts. Although immigrants and bohemian types once roamed the streets, today only the city's affluent can afford to call the crest and eastern side of the "Hill" home. At 284 feet, the views over the Bay are nothing short of stunning. The hill received its name, in fact, after the Morse Code Signal Station was built on the hill's crest in 1853. The perch had a perfect view of the whole Bay, and the station, therefore, could quickly notify downtown business interests of incoming ships. The hill was not always such a convenient place to live, hence the abundance of immigrants in the early years. All sides are incredibly steep, especially the vertiginous east side cliffs that were formed from years of quarrying. Up until 1914, the hillside was gradually carted away for landfill. Although situated in the center of the city, the hill's treacherous terrain made it seem a remote outpost, an aspect that attracted bohemian types and artists. By the 1940s, however, the area had become gentrified and steep rents forced the artists to leave. The irony: artists made the hill chic, gave it cachet, which in turn attracted the monied classes, which drove up real estate prices. At any rate, real estate prices have remained high, and Telegraph Hill remains one of the city's most affluent districts.

On these pages, aerial view of Telegraph Hill, Russian Hill and above downtown San Francisco with the Golden Gate Bridge in the distance.

FILBERT AND GREENWICH STEPS

The ubiquitous cable car, with Coit Tower in the background.

After years of plunder, the east side of Telegraph Hill became quite a sheer cliff indeed. For years when the city was first developing—and even into the twentieth century—dirt was constantly being taken from the hill. At first this dirt was used as ballast for the empty cargo hulls of Gold Rush ships, and later it was used as landfill for the city's ever-expanding downtown area. In any event, what was left of the hill's eastern face was not easily traversed. The Filbert and Greenwich steps, the pedestrian extensions of the two streets, are the best and most scenic way to tackle the hill. Over the course of thirty years a local resident, Grace Merchant, was responsible for transforming the Filbert steps from a dump heap into the beautiful, meandering landscape we see today. The homes along both stairs are some of the city's finest and most expensive, due in large part to the stunning views.

COIT TOWER

A memorial to San Francisco's volunteer firefighters, Coit Tower was constructed in 1933 at the summit of Telegraph Hill. Funds for the tower were provided by slightly daffy Lillie Hitchcock Coit, who left $100,000 towards beautifying the city upon her death in 1929.

Lillie had demonstrated a life-long obsession with fires and firefighters, so the tower seemed appropriate to commemorate both the city's eccentric benefactor as well as the platoons of San Francisco's Finest.

The 210-foot tower was designed by famed San Francisco architect Arthur Brown, who counts City Hall among his many other great projects. City lore suggests that the tower's fluted walls and porticoed observation deck were made to resemble the nozzle of a firehose. The architect, however, implored that was not his intention. Regardless, the reinforced concrete tower makes quite an impression—especially at night, when floodlights give the column an eerie, translucent quality. Sitting atop Telegraph Hill, Coit Tower has a commanding presence and can be seen from most of downtown as well as the North Bay. Likewise, in a city of many grand vistas, the view from Coit Tower's observation platform is unsurpassed.

The tower's lobby, however, is even more splendid than the views from the observation deck. The ground-floor hall is decorated floor-to-ceiling with a collection of gigantic murals that date back to the Great Depression. In 1934, the government's Works Project Administration commissioned twenty-five artists to paint the lobby. They were each paid $94 a month. The scenes offer broad interpretations of life in modern California. There are views of the city's bustling Financial District as well as images of farms, ports and factories from the farther reaches of California.

Although the styles and themes of each mural vary greatly, together they offer an incisive vision of Depression-era America. The commentaries were perhaps a bit too politically incisive, in fact, and when the murals were finished, they caused quite a stir. Before city authorities would unveil the works, several images had to be removed. Communist iconography—a hammer and sickle, for example— proved too much for a city already burdened by bloody labor strikes. Despite this censorship, the murals are an outstanding work of public art that was created by several acclaimed artists. Bernard Zakheim's *Library* should be especially noted: one of the controversial images that slipped by the censors is a worker's hand reaching for a copy of Karl Marx's infamous manifesto *Das Kapital*. Another is Victor Arnautoff's *City Life*, a detailed portrait of downtown San Francisco that shows a man being mugged at gunpoint amidst a throng of indifferent passersby.

Top, the statue of Christopher Columbus, near Coit Tower.

The famous murals in the lobby of Coit Tower date back to the Great Depression.

A cable car on Hyde Street in the Russian Hill district.

RUSSIAN HILL

With a maximum elevation of 294 feet, Russian Hill affords some of the most impressive views in the city. It is primarily a residential district that has an unusual mix of denizens. While real estate is expensive, the population maintains a somewhat bohemian flavor. As one of the most prestigious residential districts, Russian Hill has some of the premiere residential architecture. The streets are lined with beautiful homes, many in full Victorian splendor. Russian Hill purportedly got its name when the graves of Russian fur traders were discovered at the hill's summit in 1850, when the hill was still largely uninhabited. Houses were generally built at the base of the hill until 1880, when the Union Street cable-car line made Russian Hill more accessible. Telegraph Hill, North Beach and the expansive Bay can be surveyed from many points along **Vallejo Street**. On the west side of Russian Hill, Vallejo crests at Jones Street, providing an incredible panorama that can be taken in while driving along some pretty scenery. If traveling by foot, the **Vallejo Street Stairway** begins at Mason Street and climbs up through Ina Coolbrith Park. Higher still above Taylor Street are several blocks of picturesque Victorian houses. The summit of Russian Hill was one of the few areas in the city not wiped out by the catastrophe of 1906; some of the city's oldest and quaintest houses, therefore, are found here.

A nighttime view of Lombard Street ad, on the facing page, a colorful daytime image of the same picturesque street.

LOMBARD STREET

Hailed as the "crookedest street in the world," the single block of Lombard Street at the summit of Russian Hill includes eight sharp curves. For many years the hill's cobblestoned, twenty-seven-degree natural incline proved too steep for most vehicles to climb. Then in 1922 this block between Hyde and Leavenworth was revamped and the curves were added. Carl Henry, a city entrepreneur with several properties along the block, was the first to propose the corkscrew design. The block was subsequently designed with a sixteen percent grade beautified with a fancy bankment of garden planters. Today traffic flows downhill and there is a pedestrian stairway as well. The homes along this block are quite attractive and well maintained; all were built after 1940.

The neo-gothic Grace Cathedral.

NOB HILL

In the late 1870s, Robert Louis Stevenson remarked that Nob Hill was "the hill of palaces." The description was fitting over a century ago, and it is fitting now for entirely different reasons. After the invention of the cable car in 1873, the hill became a suburb of sorts, a place where the affluent could stretch out and build grandiose mansions away from the tumult of the city. All but one of the original mansions would be wiped out in 1906, of course, but new palaces would emerge.

The new palaces are not private mansions, but rather luxury hotels, exclusive clubs, an inspiring cathedral and upscale apartments and condominiums that house some of the city's wealthiest tenants.

GRACE CATHEDRAL

Fifty-three years in the making, Grace Cathedral was finally consecrated in 1964. Today it is the seat of the Episcopal bishop of California. The neo-Gothic cathedral was designed by Lewis P. Hobbart, who was trained at the Ecole des Beaux Arts in Paris. Not coincidentally, the building was modeled after thirteenth-century French cathedrals, most notably Notre Dame.

The cathedral sits on an entire block donated by renowned city benefactor Charles Crocker. When the earthquake leveled his son's mansion in 1906, Crocker gave the space to the church. The cathedral does a good job filling the lot: it is 329 feet long, 162 feet wide, and each twin belfry towers 174 feet to the heavens. One of the most spectacular aspects of the cathedral is the east entrance, where copies of Lorenzo Ghiberti's bronze *Doors of Paradise* hang. The original doors—made from the same mold—embellish the Baptistry in Florence, Italy. Inside, the stained-glass windows are transcendent. There are sixty-seven of them, the most impressive being the twenty-five-foot rose window over the entrance. Made in 1964 at the Gabriel Loire studio near Chartres, France, the *Canticle of the Sun* depicts St. Francis of Assisi's spiritual revelation. Behind the altar along the central apse, Charles Jay Connick's lovely 1931 windows portray *Christ the Light of the World* and *Christ the Good Shepherd* in brilliant shades of blue.

PACIFIC-UNION CLUB

A very private bastion of San Francisco's old-guard patriarchy, the Pacific-Union Club was formed in 1881 and remains one of the most exclusive men's social clubs in the country. The dark Connecticut brownstone building, known as the Flood mansion, was bought for $900,000 from mining magnate James Flood after the 1906 fire badly damaged the property. Londoner Augustus Laver—who won the competition to design City Hall in 1887 only to have it destroyed in the earthquake—designed Flood's Italianate, $1.5 million mansion in 1886. Because the building was made of stone and not wood, it was the only structure on Nob Hill to remain standing after the great fire. Nevertheless, it was wholly gutted, and the Flood clan subsequently migrated to Pacific Heights. The original Victorian bronze fence and gates around the property remain some of the city's finest metalwork.

29 Russell Street

According to many, 29 Russell Street is one of the most important residences in San Francisco history. This unpossessing, brown-shingled cottage that saw the creative genesis of the Beat generation was the home of Neal and Carolyn Cassady, who in 1952 offered their attic to a drifter named Jack Kerouac. It was here that Kerouac, who become the paramount Beat culture icon, wrote his three major works, *On The Road*, *Visions of Cody* and *Doctor Sax*.

29 Russell Street and, below, the Pacific Union Club.

Architect Willis Polk, one of the 450 club members, designed the building's post-fire renovation. The third story and both wings were added and the tower was lowered. In the basement, a luxurious private room was designed with Minoan columns and an illuminated, stained-glass ceiling.

HOTELS

The Fairmont Hotel — One of the city's most elegant landmarks, The Fairmont Hotel has a storied history indeed. The hotel was built on a block of land owned by Comstock millionaire James Graham Fair, whose fortunes were made mining a fifty-foot vein of silver in the Nevada hills. The hotel was built by Fair's daughter, Theresa Alice, who commissioned James and Merritt Reid to design the beautiful, 600-room Beaux Arts hotel in 1902. Just before the hotel was completed in 1906, medicine millionaires Herbert and Hartland Law bought the property from Fair. Mere months later, on April 18, the earthquake struck the city; fire gutted the building the following morning, days before it was scheduled to open. The steel-frame, terra-cotta-clad façade withstood the fire, however, and rebuilding began almost immediately. The gala celebration held on opening day was legendary. Equally legendary is the building's plush interior. Golden marble columns distinguish the lobby, which Dorothy Draper redecorated in 1947 and which has since remained a paragon of post-war elegance. **The Cirque Bar** around the corner is decorated with large, playful murals painted against a gold-leaf background. In 1962, architect Mario Gaidano added a twenty-two-story tower with an exterior glass elevator that wisks passengers to the **Fairmont Crown** lounge, the highest observation point in the city.
950 Mason Street, tel (415) 772 5000

Huntington Hotel — Built in 1924 and designed by Weeks & Day, the Huntington Hotel is one of the city's best-loved. This small, 140-room hotel stands at the very peak of Nob Hill and every room has a view of either the Bay or the city below. The Huntington was designed as a residential hotel, and it still feels rather homey. No two rooms are alike, and the milieu is elegant, charming, quaint and—most importantly—understated. There are no ostentatious displays here, no fuss. The staff is known for the longevity of its employment as well as its discretion.
1075 California Street,
tel (415) 474 5400

Ritz Carlton Hotel — A babe in the woods among Nob Hill's old-time hotels, the Ritz Carlton *(above)* has nevertheless asserted itself quite handsomely since its opening in 1991. Already this hotel has established itself as one of the city's finest. The hotel is housed in a beautiful, 1909 Beaux Arts building that fills an entire block on California Street, near the summit of the hill. There are 336 impeccably groomed rooms and all the amenities one could desire.
600 Stockton Street,
tel (415) 296 7465

Mark Hopkins Intercontinental Hotel — The Mark Hopkins Hotel, a.k.a. "The Mark," has enjoyed world renown ever since its creation in 1926. The building was designed by the architecture firm Weeks & Day, and it sits on the location of the former Mark Hopkins mansion, which was consumed by fire in 1906. In its glory, the redwood, gingerbread mansion had been the most spectacular Victorian ensemble in California. The Weeks & Day building, a brick and terra-cotta-clad Gothic Revival design, was created in many ways to commemorate the old gabled castle. The luxurious brick-paved plaza and the grand pillars at the entrance are equalled by the plush amenities inside. In 1939, the nineteenth floor was remodeled by Timothy Pfleuger and made into a cocktail lounge known far and wide as the **Top of the Mark**.
This glassed-in skyroom has 360-degree views of the Bay and surrounding hills and has been the playground of countless celebrities over the years.
1 Nob Hill, tel (415) 392 3434

Hotel Triton — A favorite haunt of young actors, art directors, designers, and creatives in general, the Triton *(above)* stands out for its eccentric decoration and for its slightly neo-Hippy atmosphere. Not by chance there's a suite named after Jerry Garcia, the leader of the legendary Grateful Dead, and a number of "Zen Dens," rooms which while quite small are also quite comfortable and tastefully furnished. Services, besides the 24-hour gym, include nightly wine parties in front of the fireplace and tarot readings. Located near Union Square, the Triton is the ideal place to stay, whether you're in SF for business or for pleasure.
342 Grant Avenue, tel (415) 394 0500, www.hotel-tritonsf.com.

Archbishop's Mansion Inn — The former San Francisco bishopric, at the northeast corner of Alamo Square, has been transformed into a luxury bed-and-breakfast in Belle Époque style. Some of the rooms have Jacuzzi tubs and fireplaces. The leaded glass dome over the lobby is magnificent.
1000 Fulton Street,
tel (415) 563 7872

View of downtown San Francisco from Twin Peaks.

TWIN PEAKS

Once known as *Los Pechos de la Chola, The Breasts of the Indian Girl,* the Twin Peaks are the city's second- and third-tallest hills, both topping 900 feet. The 360-degree views from the top of Twin Peaks are incredible, especially at night when the lights of the city are ablaze below. When Daniel Burnham needed a look-out post from which to survey and plan the city in 1905, he came to Twin Peaks. Today Twin Peaks is a residential district with some of the city's largest properties.

There is a bit more elbow room here, and many of the homes have gardens and lush landscaping. Twin Peaks Boulevard wraps around both hills and offers some great vistas.

POTRERO HILL DISTRICT

A quiet, sleepy residential district, Potrero Hill overlooks The Mission District to the west and downtown San Francisco to the north. Like The Mission, Potrero Hill was an early suburb, joined to the city by a five-mile stretch of cable-car tracks. The area enjoys the city's sunniest climate and sports some lovely colorful houses. It has now become home to many good restaurants and shops. Among the neighborhood's claims to fame, Vermont Street is nearly as curvaceous as Russian Hill's Lombard Street—but the turns are even more hair-raising and heart-stopping. Anchor Steam Brewery on Mariposa Street, founded in 1851 to quench gold diggers' thirsts, is the city's choice beer maker.

Sure to please all small children, **Basic Brown Bears** is a small stuffed-animal factory that specializes in—can you guess?—teddy bears. The factory offers a free thirty minute tour, after which shoppers can buy and stuff their own loveable teddy bears.

SHOWPLACE SQUARE

At the foot of Potrero Hill among a host of other restored nineteenth-century warehouses stands Showplace Square, one of the largest wholesale furniture centers in the country. Open to the trade, these showrooms offer furniture and interior decoration in just about every conceivable style. The **Design Center** within the square consists of two warehouses linked by a modern, glass atrium used for exhibitions and conventions.

Two views of the Potrero Hill district and, bottom, the SF Design Center on Showplace Square.

ALONG THE COAST

A view toward the city and the Presidio National Park.
Bottom, two lovely views of the Golden Gate Bridge
from a lookout near Chrissy Field in the Presidio
National Park.

THE PRESIDIO

The Presidio was founded by the Spanish in 1776 to guard the entrance to San Francisco Bay. The original installation was a hundred-yard-square camp surrounded by a palisade wall. When the Mexicans gained independence in 1822, they took over the site. When the United States annexed California in 1846, the Presidio became a U.S. military base. When the base was recently closed, it had been the longest-serving military base in the country. Union soldiers trained here during the Civil War, and during World War II it was a significant army headquarters. Planted with pine and eucalyptus trees in the 1880s, the 1,446-acre Presidio includes the largest tract of forest in the city, the majority of which is part of the **Golden Gate National Recreation Area.** Unspoiled nature is the big draw here today, as beautiful sprawling paths cut through the forest and offer panoramic views. The Presidio is to become the largest urban National Park in the United States.

Top, the Montgomery Barracks.

THE PRESIDIO ARMY MUSEUM

B uilt in 1863 and formerly the Old Station Hospital, the Army Museum is the oldest surviving building in the Presidio. The museum is surrounded by defunct artillery. Inside is a vast collection of memorabilia recounting the army's history in the Bay Area, including old uniforms and weapons, portraits and early photographs, wartime propaganda and strategic maps and charts. The museum has a strong bent towards the nineteenth century, when the army played an important role in taming the West.

*Above, an ornate cannon
and, right,
the Presidio Army Museum.*

FORT POINT

A thrilling Civil War relic, Fort Point resides under the southern arch of the Golden Gate Bridge. The fort was built by Union forces between 1853 and 1861 to protect the entrance of San Francisco Bay. The staunch, massive brick fort was built a mere ten feet above the encroaching sea, lending the building a courageous and defiant attitude. Although the fort was furnished with 126 cannons and a vast arsenal, not a single shot was ever fired from here in defense of the city. The fort's thick walls are built around a vaulted-brick courtyard that is accessed through monolithic, studded doors. Inside are living quarters and a garrison that have been converted into a museum featuring vintage photographs, uniforms and weapons.

The parapets facing the bay, usually braced by cold, stiff winds, offer an incredible view of the Golden Gate Bridge above and the city behind.

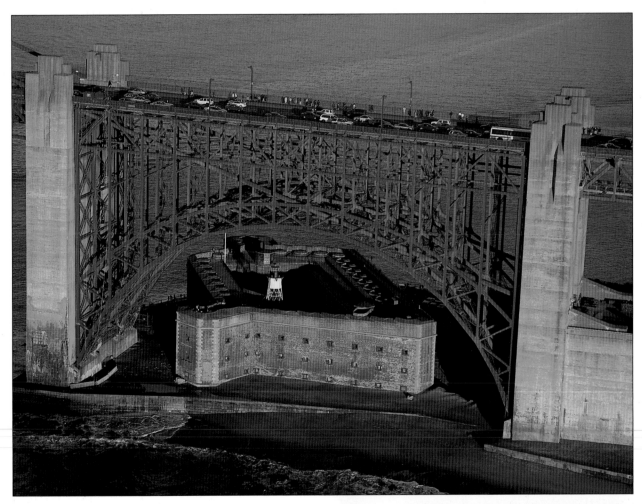

Above: the 19th-century Fort Point seems very small between two pylons under the south span of the Golden Gate Bridge. Right: the Pet Cemetery.

Pet Cemetery — Tucked away off Crissy Field Avenue behind a quaint white picket fence, the pet cemetery that has proliferated in recent years was originally reserved for military animals and pets only. Civilians have apparently infringed upon the picturesque setting to lay their four-legged loved ones to rest, sharing these sacred grounds with such courageous national heroes as General Pershing's horse.

FORT MASON AND NORTHERN WATERFRONT

Western frontier headquarters for the U.S. army in the mid-nineteenth century and a pivotal command post during World War II, Fort Mason is today one of the city's most important cultural centers. With over fifty cultural organizations spread over this bayside parkland, including several museums, theaters and galleries, Fort Mason has made the transition to civilian life quite smoothly.

The land was originally residential property until Union soldiers took it over in the 1850s to construct an army compound. Seeing the manicured lawns of the **Great Meadow** today, it is hard to imagine that 1.6 million soldiers embarked from Fort Mason to fight in the Pacific during World War II.

The base was demilitarized in 1972, and since then it has become a significant art and cultural mecca. The fort's barracks and warehouses have been converted into an arts complex called the **Fort Mason Center**.

In an effort to promote Latino cultures in the U.S., the **Mexican Museum** here collects and exhibits a broad range of modern and traditional arts of Mexicans and Mexican-Americans. The Museum plans to open its permanent home in the Yerba Buena Gardens neighborhood in 2003.

Another well-established resource center, the **African-American Historical and Cultural Society** includes a library and gallery space used to exhibit works by contemporary African-Americans and also to recount the history of African-American pioneers in the Bay Area. Established to celebrate

Fort Mason: the Marina, the statue of Philip Burton, and the GGNRA (Golden Gate National Recreation Area) headquarters.

the identity of one of the city's earliest and most prominent ethnic communities, the **Museo Italo-Americano** stages a wide variety of historical and cultural exhibitions. The widely-acclaimed **San Francisco Craft & Folk Art Museum** displays and sells handmade crafts from around the world.

The **San Francisco Museum of Modern Art** rental gallery is also in the park, as is the **San Francisco Maritime Historical Library**. Some of the city's finest experimental theater is staged at Fort Mason as well, and walks along the 3.5-mile **Golden Gate Promenade**, which cuts through the compound along rocky cliffs, are enjoyed by locals and tourists alike.

FORT MASON HIGHLIGHTS

MUSEUM OF CRAFT AND FOLK ART

Located in Building A of the Fort Mason complex, this arts and crafts museum is the only one of its kind on the West Coast. Although it has been open for almost twenty years now, it does not possess a permanent collection but by choice remains a completely dynamic space where visitors will find continually-changing exhibits designed to stimulate curiosity concerning the so-called "minor" arts and provide understanding of their intricacies. The original exhibits presented by this museum are in fact an open invitation to stretching the conventional definition of "art," since they point up the artistic content to be found even in the humblest of objects for everyday use. The theme areas range from contemporary American crafts to the traditional ethnic art of exotic cultures like that of Japan or the Australian aborigines. Each exhibit is accompanied by conferences and seminars open to the public, while at the gift shop visitors may purchase the catalogues of all the most popular exhibits ever organized by the museum.

*Center:
Michail Lucero,* Vessel Form Representing a Growling Terrier *(1994). Clay with glazes.*

Top left:Jean William Caicedo, Hunting Coat. *Wool, dye, pieced.*

Above: Anonymous, Rio Grande Blanket *(1885-95). Wool, 50" x 77".*
Rachel Porter, Yellow Bowl. *Ceramic. Bowls (1993) from Mpingo (Africa).*

SAN FRANCISCO AFRICAN AMERICAN HISTORICAL AND CULTURAL SOCIETY

Founded in 1855 by the merger of the San Francisco Negro Historical Society and the local chapter of the Association for the Study of Negro Life and History, the SFAAHCS is one of the oldest institutions of its kind. This cultural center and museum sponsors research on the history of the Afro-American population, and promotes past and present Afro-American art. The exhibit space in Building C at Fort Mason hosts interdisciplinary exhibits of the traditional art and culture of various African and Afro-American populations as well as exhibits of the work of individual Afro-American artists. The gift shop has a broad selection of art.

An-step Back Sally and Summer Silk, *by Hilda Robinson.*

Ongandjera Woman and Mangbetu Woman *by Hillary Younglove.*

Two photographs by David Johns.

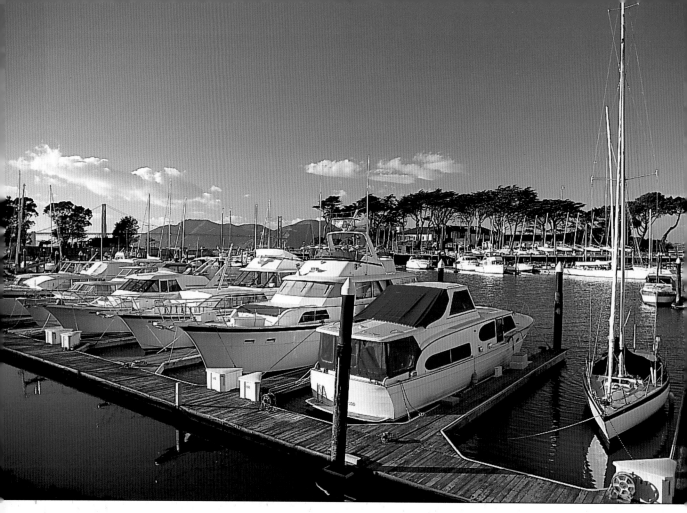

Marina District, the San Francisco Yacht Club.

THE MARINA

The Marina District is a flat residential neighborhood built largely on landfill, which accounts for its poor showing in the 1989 Loma Prieta earthquake. Much Marina housing was damaged in that quake and several homes were subsequently lost to fire. The Marina and SOMA, in fact, were the neighborhoods hardest hit by Loma Prieta. Nevertheless, the Marina has rebounded from the quake and has again been restored to a quiet, affluent, pastel-colored neighborhood. The buildings reflects the Italianate architecture popular in the 1920s, when many of these houses were built.

Between Divisadero and Fillmore, **Chestnut Street** is the Marina's main shopping street and the new hot spot for young urban professionals to wine and dine. Despite being one of the city's trendiest locales, Chestnut Street remains a rather quaint stretch of restaurants, cafes and boutiques that has so far managed to avoid tacky commercialization.

Time may be running out for Chestnut Street, however, as its newfound celebrity threatens its small-town charm.

MARINA GREEN PARK

A narrow park that stretches along the Yacht Harbor with a tremendous bay view, Marina Green is the neighborhood playground. Many residents of this affluent enclave, in fact, have boats docked in front. When not testing their sea legs, locals come to Marina Green to exercise, fly kites, relax and generally see and be seen. The west end of Marina Green features a **wave organ**, a most unusual musical instrument. Best heard at high tide, the organ's jumble of pipes were designed to whine and belch as waves hit it.

FISHERMAN'S WHARF

The city's most popular tourist attraction, Fisherman's Wharf was given its carnival façade in the late 1970s and hasn't looked back since. Chinese fishermen first settled here back in the city's earliest days, followed by the Italians in the late nineteenth century. The piers were stocked with colorful boats and the fishing commerce was swift and easy until the mid-twentieth century. After World War II, the bay became increasingly polluted and fishing in northern California became overly competitive. The fishing trade dropped off, and the piers fell into neglect. To reinvigorate the area, the shipping piers and surrounding streets were transformed into a tourist haven. The streets are lined with such thrilling amusements as the **Guinness Museum of World Records** and **Ripley's Believe It or Not! Museum**, making Fisherman's Wharf a gaudy spectacle, but one not to be missed. Having sunk six enemy vessels and damaged countless others in World War II, the **USS Pampanito Submarine** now resides at Pier 45 in Fisherman's Wharf. Tours of the Pampanito today travel from bow to stern, passing through the torpedo room, bridge and cramped sleeping quarters and creating a vivid feeling of claustrophobia.

Neon signs reflect in the dark waters around Fisherman's Wharf at night.

Fisherman's Wharf, an important point of reference for the fishing trade.

Opposite, pictures of the crowded Fisherman's Wharf.

The Cannery, once the headquarters of the Del Monte Fruit Company, and the white Dolphin Club building.

THE CANNERY

Following the factory-converting success of Ghirardelli Square, The Cannery building was renovated in 1968 by Joseph Esherick & Associates. Constructed in 1909 by Philip Bush, the original three-story building housed the Del Monte Fruit Company's peach-canning plant. Designed around a sunken courtyard filled with flowers and street performers, the building today contains a comedy club, a movie theater and several galleries, restaurants and shops.

PIER 39

The centerpiece of Fisherman's Wharf, Pier 39 was converted into a glitzy, faux-eighteenth-century New England wharf in 1978. After Walt Disney's two fun parks, Pier 39 is the most-visited amusement attraction in the country. The complex includes two levels of shops, restaurants and amusements that cater to every tourist whim. A ride in the **double-deck carousel** is a favorite among young children, as is **Aquarium of the Bay**, a 50,000-square-foot aquarium that presents a vast array of northern California's indigenous marine life. A high-tech multimedia show, **The Great San Francisco Adventure** is a 30-minute movie and gives an impressive overview of what the city is all about. Although the uninvited horde of barking **sea lions** has become one of the Pier's strongest attractions, the street performers are pretty entertaining as well. The **Blue and Gold Fleet** ferry departs from Pier 39 and gives sight-seeing tours of the bay.

Sea lions frolicking in the pier and, below, an aerial view of Pier 39 and Fisherman's Wharf,

A panoramic birds-eye view of Pier 39, with a historic trolley on the road.

Historical and new vessels docked at Fisherman's Wharf; bottom, the Balclutha, *built in 1883.*

Opposite, Ghirardelli Square by night.

GHIRARDELLI SQUARE

The most attractive commercial complex in Fisherman's Wharf, Ghirardelli Square houses many fine stores, restaurants, galleries and other places to browse. During the mid-nineteenth century, Ghirardelli Square was the site of a wool mill, although the most famous resident and namesake of the square was the Ghirardelli Chocolate Factory. Built by Domenico Ghirardelli in 1900, many of the factory's original, red-brick buildings still remain, as does the landmark sign on the roof and several of the original chocolate-making machines.
Setting a precedent in urban renewal across the country, the factory's conversion was designed by Wurster, Bernardi & Emmons architects and Lawrence Halprin & Associates landscape architects in 1962. The space is a pleasant one through which to meander, with several wide plazas and winding walkways. Street performers entertain throughout the square and, among the many other interesting sites, the **Ghirardelli Chocolate Factory** still produces luscious candy bars and old-fashioned ice cream.

EMBARCADERO CENTER

The Embarcadero Center is an urban sprawl of landscaped plazas, patios, walkways and bridges that connect four slim, modern towers and cover almost eight square blocks. The center, as well as the four surrounding high-rises, was designed by John Portman and Associates in 1982. Since that time three more buildings have been added. In all, the center houses more than 120 stores, cafés and restaurants that are arranged in a comfortable setting. The center's design is user-friendly, and the outdoor spaces are well conceived.

Although the Embarcadero is mainly commercial in scope, the boulevards linking the various building that make up the complex are studded with sculptures by contemporary artists of international renown. Untitled, the German artist Franz Koenig's *bronze globe* decorated with modern hieroglyphics, stands at the corner of Commercial and Battery Streets, and at **Two Embarcadero Center** it's hard not to note the enormous and hugely fascinating Chronos XIV by the French-Hungarian Nicholas Schoffer. Finally, a not-to-be-foregone experience is a cocktail at eye-level with the Center's scintillating towers, at the elegant revolving Equinox bar atop the Hyatt Regency Hotel.

Embarcadero Center: a historic trolley stop and, below, a general view of the waterfront by night.

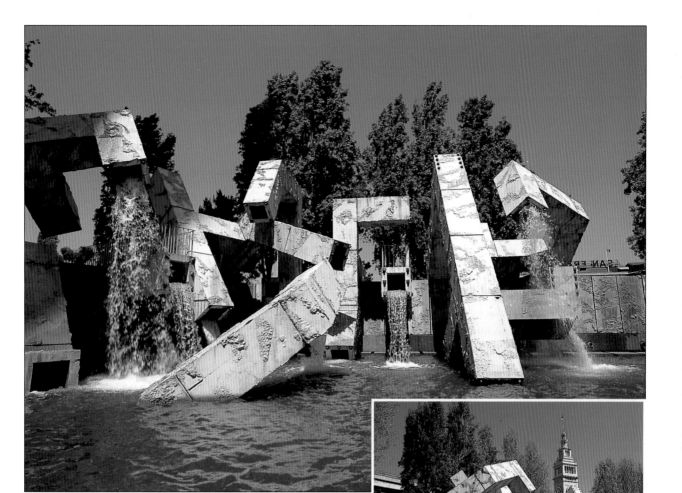

Justin Herman Plaza: the Vaillancourt Fountain.

VAILLANCOURT FOUNTAIN

Designed by Canadian artist Armand Vaillancourt in 1971, the gargantuan Vaillancourt Fountain erupts dramatically from the center of Justin Herman Plaza. This avant-garde structure is considered quite ugly by many, although most admit that it is provocative and intriguing to look at. A convoluted jumble of concrete blocks and metal girders jutting from pools at drastic angles, the fountain spouts grand sheets and columns of water. During frequent times of drought, the fountain unfortunately remains dry.

FERRY BUILDING

One of the few downtown buildings left standing after the 1906 earthquake, the Ferry Building survived only through the yeomen efforts of fireboats pumping water from the bay. Designed by Arthur Page Brown in 1894 and completed in 1903, the Ferry Building served as the gateway to the city before the advent of the Bay and Golden Gate Bridges in 1937, when ferries were the only practical means of transportation to the city. At one point it was the second busiest gateway in the world: 170 daily ferries ushered in fifty million passengers to the city every year, most of whom were daily commuters from Oakland and Marin County.

At 235 feet tall, the Ferry Building was for many years the tallest structure in the city, a proud beacon for travelers across the bay. Besides the stately clock tower, the building's elegant architecture sports lovely colonnades and internal arcades. The building was modeled after the Moorish belltower of the Giralda Cathedral Tower in Seville, Spain.

Remarkably, the building survived the Loma Prieta earthquake of 1989 unscathed, even though the quake did extensive damage to the Embarcadero Freeway that separates the bay-front building from the rest of the city. After construction of the city's bridges, the building fell largely to disuse. Today only a few ferries come and go each day, and the building is the home of the city's port authority and world trade center. A relic from the D-Day invasion, the **SS Jeremiah O'Brien** anchored along the Embarcadero near the Ferry Building is the last of the Liberty Ships launched during World War II. The ship recently returned from a historic voyage to Europe for a celebration commemorating the end of World War II.

Several suggestive images of the SF-Oakland Bay Bridge, which spans more than 4 miles (7 km) of San Francisco Bay.

SAN FRANCISCO-OAKLAND BAY BRIDGE

The longest steel structure in the world, the Bay Bridge was also one of the costliest ever built. The dream team of engineers Charles Purcell, Charles Andrew, Glenn Woodruff and architect Timothy Pfleuger designed the project during the depths of the Great Depression.

The four-mile structure is actually made up of two bridges: the cantilever section is one, the suspension span is technically two separate bridges joined in the middle at the Center Anchorage. Four miles of the bridge hover over the Bay, 190 feet below, by a tunnel through Yerba Buena Island, which at the time was the world's widest.

The two-level bridge is a complex structure that employs a cantilever design on the Oakland side and a double-suspension design on the San Francisco side. While the lower deck was originally designed to transport electric trains, today each level has five car lanes that usher 280,000 motorists on their way every day. The project took three years to build and was finally opened in 1936. The New Deal Reconstruction Finance Corporation footed the $70 million bill. These sections are supported xby massive piers that are, quite literally, whithout peers. The bridge itself swallowed eighteen percent of the steel produced in the United States in 1933.

During the 1989 Loma Prieta earthquake, a frightening accident occurred when a section of the bridge's upper deck collapsed onto the lower, killing one person, Amazingly, a herculan construction effort kept the bridge closed for only bone month.

ALCATRAZ

Alcatraz Island, known as "The Rock."

Today, Alcatraz is no less a wind swept, forlorn place as when it held some of the country's best known and most feared criminals. Although the prisoners have long abandoned the island, "The Rock" continues to hold a special place in the imagination of the public.

Since becoming part of the National Park System's **Golden Gate National Recreation Area** in 1972, Alcatraz has become one of the Bay Area's most popular destinations. Ferry boats carry nearly one million visitors to Alcatraz each year. Once on the island, visitors are free to walk around designated areas, join a guided tour led by **Park Rangers,** take a self-guided, audio-cassette tour of the cellhouse, visit the bookstore within the old military barracks, browse exhibits and watch a short informative documentary on the history of the island.

Access to many sections of the island is limited due to hazardous conditions caused by demolished and deteriorating structures. The **National Park System**, with the help of the non-profit **Golden Gate National Park Association**, is slowly opening more of the island to visitors, who are rewarded with spectacular views of **San Francisco Bay**, the city of **San Francisco** and the **Golden Gate Bridge**.

The island sits directly in the path of the fog bearing, chilly westerly winds that blow through the Golden Gate, particularly during summer afternoons. Coming prepared for a visit to Alcatraz means carrying a sweater or a jacket. Also bring comfortable walking shoes, as many paths are steep. Visitors can spend the entire day on the island, but must return with the last ferry to San Francisco (the schedule varies according to season).

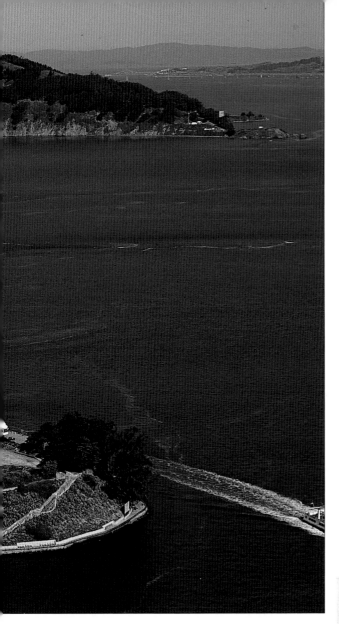

island was called *La Isla de los Alcatraces*, after a species of cormorants found in Spain. There was no fresh water on the island and the only vegetation was some hardy grass that managed to grow out of the limestone. It was not until California became a part of the United States that Alcatraz began to change.

In 1853, the U.S. Army decided to build an impregnable defensive fortress on Alcatraz to protect the city of San Francisco and the Bay. At the same time, work began on the first West Coast lighthouse. Large parts of the island were blasted away to make room for the fort and gun emplacements. Tons of soil were also brought over from Angel Island, which today supports the lush vegetation that grows on sections of Alcatraz.

While the island's fire power was never tested, its security as a prison soon was. Starting in 1861, only two years after the island opened as a military fortress, Alcatraz began receiving **Civil War prisoners** and for the next decades the island was both a fort and a military prison. By 1910 Alcatraz was only a military prison and work was under way on the present cellhouse and lighthouse. The U.S. Army pulled out of Alcatraz altogether in 1934, but the island did not remain vacant. In August of that year, Alcatraz became an ultra maximum-security Federal Penitentiary. A crime wave had been sweeping the country during the years of Prohibition and Great Depression and the federal government was looking for a secure place to imprison notorious gangsters and recalcitrant prisoners serving time in other Federal Penitentiaries. Thus, Alcatraz became home to **Al Capone**, **George "Machine Gun" Kelly** and **Robert Stroud**, the **"Birdman of Alcatraz."**

Right, above: famous "guests" of Alcatraz included Robert "Birdman" Stroud, interested in bird diseases, and "Machine Gun" Kelly.
Right, below: Harmon Waley being escorted to Alcatraz in April, 1934; Al "Scarface" Capone.

Although the ferry service is frequent, tickets sell out quickly, especially in the summer. Therefore, it is a good idea to purchase tickets in advance. The island played an important role in the formative years of the city of San Francisco and the state of California. Alcatraz was the sight of the **first lighthouse** built on the West Coast, and was also an important **military fort** protecting San Francisco Bay.

Alcatraz continues to be best known for its 29 years as America's **ultra maximum security** prison, but visitors should also become acquainted with the interesting early years of the island's heritage. The early buildings and history of Alcatraz are not as visible as the main cellblock, or as dramatic as the tales of the famous prisoners and the escape attempts, but they are just as compelling. The island received its name in 1775, when Spanish explorers charted San Francisco Bay. The rocky

Alcatraz Federal Penitentiary, too expensive to maintain and its physical infrastructure deteriorating was closed in 1963. No one knew what to do with the island until, after the **Native American occupation** of 1969-1971, it became part of the new **Golden Gate National Recreation Area** in 1972.

BROADWAY AND A, B, C, D-BLOCKS

One of the features of Alcatraz that attracted Department of Justice officials in the early 1930s was the relatively modern cellhouse, which had been built by the U.S. Army between 1909 and 1912. The cellhouse was one of the largest reinforced concrete structures of its time. The four cellblocks: A, B, C, and D, contained 600 cells on three tiers. The cellblocks stood within the cellhouse, so that no cell adjoined with an outside wall. If a convict somehow managed to tunnel though his cell wall, he was still inside the main prison building.
When the first warden of the Federal Penitentiary, **James A. Johnston**, was asked to oversee the works that would make Alcatraz escape proof, he decided that the prisoners would be confined to B- and C-Blocks, since the prisoner population was not to exceed 300. Therefore, the cells in these two blocks underwent several modifications, while the cells in A-Block remained unaltered. Two of the most important improvements undertaken were the replacement of the softer flat iron bars (which could be more easily pried open) with thicker hardened steel bars and the

installation of a new centralized cell locking system. This new system allowed any number of selected cells to be opened and locked simultaneously.
The main corridor dividing B- and C-Blocks was dubbed **"Broadway"** and the open area at the north end of the cellblock that led into the dining hall was called **"Times Square."** "Broadway," especially the ground floor, contained the least desirable cells. They were colder, had less privacy and were darker than the other cells. New inmates spent a month in quarantine in "Broadway." White and black prisoners were segregated up until the last years of the prison's operations.
D-Block contained forty-two cells and there was an ascending scale of punishment severity, from Isolation to Solitary to the Strip Cell. Isolation consisted of thirty-six cells, which were identical to those of the regular cell blocks. The difference was that inmates in Isolation remained in the cells twenty-four hours a day. They took their meals there and were allowed one shower (fifteen minutes) per week and given one hour per week in the exercise yard. One of the ways a prisoner could be sent to Isolation was to be so disagreeable or unstable that he had to be kept apart from the general inmate population. This was the case with **Robert Stroud, "The Birdman of Alcatraz."**
The very end of the line was the Strip Cell, there was only one. As with Solitary, the Strip Cell was completely dark. In addition, there was neither a toilet nor sink, only a hole in the floor and the cell itself was not the only thing stripped. Prisoners were frequently put in naked, usually as punishment for destruction of their clothes, mattresses, or blankets. Time in the Strip Cell

On pages 144-145: Alcatraz Island today, looking south towards the skyline of San Francisco.

"Broadway" between B Block and C- Block.

was generally brief, usually two days.

A-Block never housed inmates while Alcatraz was a Federal Penitentiary and in fact was never modernized for this purpose. Therefore, with its flat strap-iron bars, key locks and spiral staircases, it is the only example of the original cellblocks that were built when the island was a military prison. A-Block was used sparingly, but occasionally, troublemakers would be placed there, as would prisoners awaiting a hearing or a transfer. Starting in the late 1940s, prisoners were allowed to use the cells in A-Block to type documents, such as legal briefs for their lawyers. Some of the cells on this block also feature graffti left behind by some of the prisoners temporarily housed in this portion of the cellhouse.

Top, inmates lining up for work details in the recreation yard in the 1950s and, above, for a meal in Alcatraz's last years as Federal Penitentiary.

The "Bay to Breakers" annual race is run on a 73/4 mile (12.5 km) course from the Ferry Building to Ocean Beach.

GOLDEN GATE PARK

Once an embarrassment to the city, a stretch of briny, infertile land that nay-sayers believed impregnable to cultivation, Golden Gate Park is today a paragon of urban landscape architecture. When invited by the city to offer his expertise, Frederick Law Olmstead, architect of New York City's Central Park, deemed the Golden Gate Park project impossible. William Hammond Hall, on the other hand, had a vision. He designed the park in 1866, and work began in 1871 with the creation of the Panhandle. Hall's original plan aside, the man most responsible for the park's triumphant

success was John McLaren, the young Scotsman who became superintendent of gardening in 1890. For over fifty years until his death in 1943, McLaren cultivated the land, planting first grass and small shrubs to solidify the ground and then larger bushes and trees. Over his career, he was responsible for planting over a million trees, many of which grew up to eighty feet tall. McLaren's statue stands at the entrance to **Rhododendron Dell**. Today the park indeed feels far removed from the strains and stresses of the city. Paved walkways meander through the landscape of flowers, meadows, lakes, hills and forests. The **Strybing Arboretum** alone includes over 6,000 species of trees, plants and shrubs, some indigenous to northern California and others imported. Plants are selected for their taste,

146

touch and smell, with one garden dedicated to the olfactory senses alone. The **Shakespeare Garden**, on the other hand, features only those flowers and plants alluded to in the Great Bard's sonnets and plays, with the relevant quotes written on plaques set in a wall at the back of the garden. Marked by the large Dutch windmill built in the park's northwest corner in 1903, the **Queen Wilhelmina Tulip Garden** features a colorful array of tulips that bloom each spring. A much woolier experience, the thirty-five-acre **Buffalo Paddock** was opened in 1892 and is currently home to fourteen shaggy American bison, the largest animals on North American soil. In addition to the flower gardens and sanctuaries, there are countless playing fields as well as a host of highly respected museums and cultural centers.

The Queen Wilhelmina Tulip Garden with the ancient Dutch Windmill, one of the pumping stations built to irrigate Golden Gate Park.

Below, the Dahlia Garden.

THE CONSERVATORY OF FLOWERS

Constructed by Lord and Burnham in 1878, the Conservatory is the oldest building in the park. Inspired by the Palm House at Kew Gardens in London, the structure's frame was actually built in Dublin and shipped around Cape Horn. Eccentric millionaire James Lick commissioned the ornate glasshouse building—which miraculously survived two major earthquakes—but did not live to see it constructed.

The Conservatory displays a collection of tropical plants and orchids and has special flower shows each season. The stunning gardens surrounding the Conservatory are filled with flowers and flowering trees.

At the moment the building is under renovation because of the damages caused by recent years' rough weather and it is scheduled to reopen in the near future.

JAPANESE TEA GARDEN

The Japanese Tea Garden is one of the crown jewels of Golden Gate Park. Built by art dealer George Marsh for the California Midwinter International Exposition of 1894, the garden was preserved by park overlord John McLaren after the exposition ended. Prominent gardeners, the Hagiwara family took charge of the garden until World War II, when they were sent to internment camps along with 110,000 other Japanese-Americans living in northern California. Today the garden is a perfect blend of nature and architecture. Bridges, footpaths, statuary and gates meld seamlessly into the natural landscape of trees, flowers and streams. When the cherry trees bloom in April, the garden is ablaze in soft pinks and white. Cast in Japan in 1790, an eleven-foot bronze **Buddha**—the largest outside of Asia—sits at the top of a set of garden stairs. Another impressive monument, the **Shinto Pagoda** is a five-tiered wooden shrine. Along with its reflection in the pond below, the steeply arched **Wishing Bridge** forms a perfect circle when viewed from above.

On these pages, period photographs of the Conservatory of Flowers and Japanese Tea Garden.

Below and opposite page, top: splendid views of the Japanese Tea Garden in Golden Gate Park.

Tea Garden
G.G. Park S.F.

149

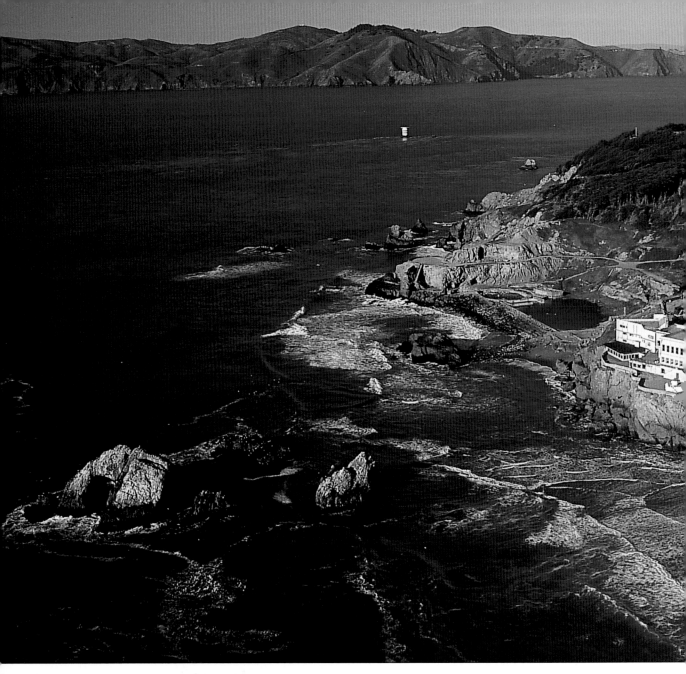

An aerial view of the Cliff House.

Period photographs.
Left, Sutro Baths.
   Opposite, from top to bottom: Sutro Baths, interior;
the SS Pennsylvania, the "Golden Gate," and Fort Point;
a view of the beach, the Seal Rocks, the Cliff House, and
Sutro Heights.

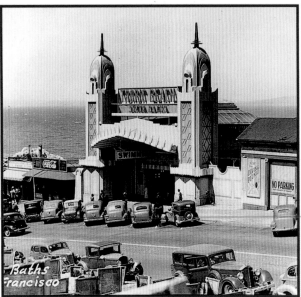

CLIFF HOUSE

A mere shadow of its former self, the Cliff House today houses a restaurant that sheds little light on the building's storied past. The original Cliff House was built back in 1863 as a ocean-side retreat for the city's affluent. Over the years the resort became a reputed mob hang out. On Christmas Day in 1894, the building burned down. The following year, Comstock millionaire Adolph Sutro built a Gothic wooden castle on the site and opened it as a family resort. Next to the building he opened the **Sutro Baths**, a three-acre spa

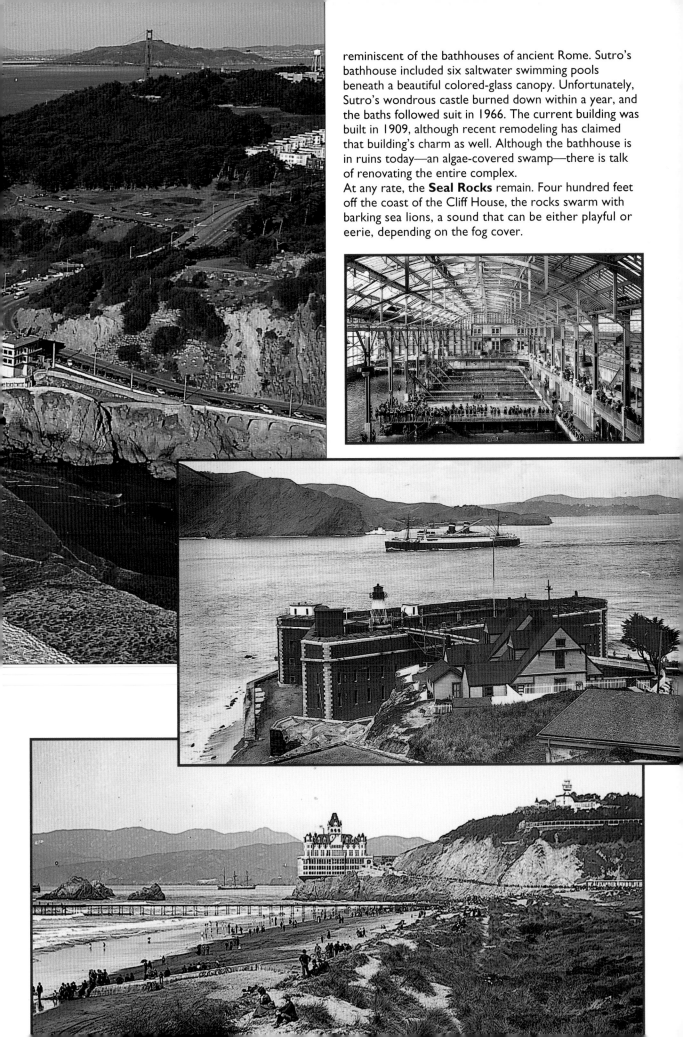

reminiscent of the bathhouses of ancient Rome. Sutro's bathhouse included six saltwater swimming pools beneath a beautiful colored-glass canopy. Unfortunately, Sutro's wondrous castle burned down within a year, and the baths followed suit in 1966. The current building was built in 1909, although recent remodeling has claimed that building's charm as well. Although the bathhouse is in ruins today—an algae-covered swamp—there is talk of renovating the entire complex.

At any rate, the **Seal Rocks** remain. Four hundred feet off the coast of the Cliff House, the rocks swarm with barking sea lions, a sound that can be either playful or eerie, depending on the fog cover.

LINCOLN PARK

I n Lincoln Park at the northwest corner of the San Francisco peninsula, the visitor will thrill to a spectacular itinerary over the shore cliffs that run from Lands End to Point Lobos.

The park offers a number of different attractions, like the city golf course, the USS San Francisco memorial, the ruins of Fort Miley, and the Sutro Baths, in the Victorian era the largest spa complex in the entire world.

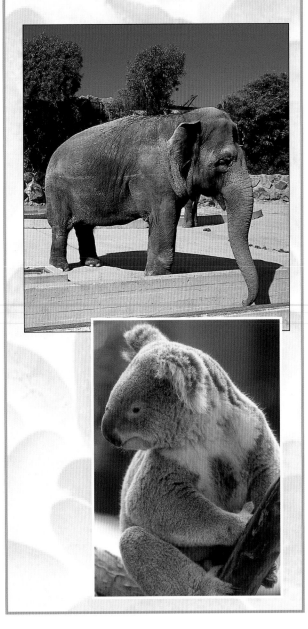

A view of the Lincoln Park Golf Course.

Two guests of the San Francisco Zoo.

SAN FRANCISCO ZOO

Opened in 1929, the San Francisco Zoo covers sixty-five acres of parkland in the city's far southwest corner, between the Pacific Ocean and Lake Merced. The zoo has over 1,000 species of birds and mammals, thirty of which are considered to be endangered. Natural habitats are gradually replacing the concrete cages with metal bars. A good example of the trend is Gorilla World, one of the world's largest naturalistic zoo settings. Koala Crossing is another highlight, designed to be like the Australian outback. The Lion House is the site of bloody carnage most days at 2PM, when the big cats are fed. The innovative Primate Discovery Center features interactive computer programs that describe the monkeys and apes. The Children's Zoo features a host of animals that like to be petted.

A view of the Yerba Buena Gardens.

SOUTH OF MARKET

S OMA, the area South of Market Street, is the city's most eclectic neighborhood. Back in the 1850s, before the advent of the cable car lured the affluent to Nob Hill to build their mansions, Rincon Hill was one of the most prestigious addresses in the city. Beginning in 1883, however, Market Street became one of the main cable-car thoroughfares and, in the process, became a distinct social dividing line. The area "South of the Slot," as the cable conduit on Market was known, became an increasingly working-class neighborhood, while the region to the north developed into a solid middle- and upper-class neighborhood. After the 1906 quake leveled the area south of Market, factories, train yards and warehouses were constructed. For the next seventy years, SOMA remained industrial and rather oppressive. Industry eventually moved away, however, and in the 1970s and 1980s artists and musicians began to convert the large factory spaces into studios and living quarters. The area has gotten progressively more gentrified ever since. Today the area has a world-class cultural center, a spiffy new museum, a convention center, trendy restaurants, bars and clubs, a flower market and several popular retail outlets, not to mention attractive new residential developments.

YERBA BUENA GARDENS

T hirty years in the planning, the Yerba Buena Center project was begun to promote the city's diverse artistic community. Opened in 1993, the $87 million center features several first-rate facilities, including the **Visual Arts Center**, **Yerba Buena Gardens** and the **Esplanade**. The Visual Arts Center is the first work in the United States designed by cutting-edge Japanese architect Fumihiko Maki. The façade is dark and industrial-looking, with sections of corrugated metal siding. Inside the center offers 55,000 square feet of gallery space and a sculpture court that exhibit contemporary art. Across the way, **Yerba Buena Theater** was designed by New York architect James Stewart Polshek and features a 750-seat theater reserved for the use of nonprofit companies. There is also an outdoor stage with lawn seating that can accommodate 3,000. Between the arts center and the theater, the Esplanade unifies the whole Yerba Buena project. The centerpiece is the **Martin Luther King Memorial,** a twenty-foot-high, fifty-foot-wide, Sierra granite waterfall designed by sculptor Houston Conwell. Illuminated glass panels are inscribed with the fallen civil rights leader's inspiring words. All around the green lawn there are many activities for kids such as: an ice-skating rink, a bowling alley, a historic **Carousel** from 1906 and the **Zeum**, wich is an interactive cultural center geared specifically for children and teenagers.

MOSCONE CONVENTION CENTER

San Francisco's primary convention hall, the Moscone Center occupies close to three city blocks and boasts over one million square feet of useable space. Designed by Hellmuth, Obata and Kassabaum in 1981, the convention center is the centerpiece of the Yerba Buena Gardens project. It was named after Mayor George Moscone, who was assassinated by disgruntled ex-supervisor Dan White on November 28, 1978. The subterranean exhibit hall covers 300,000 square feet and is an impressive architectural feat. Engineered by T.Y. Lin, the hall boasts an astounding system of supports that makes interior columns unnecessary. Incredibly, the arched roof is

SOMA: the Moscone Convention Center with its more than 1,000,000 square feet of useable space.

supported by a network of steel cables that runs under the floor. The result is a vast, expansive space, one of the largest underground spaces in the world. Despite being largely underground, the convention center employs an imaginative array of skylights and artificial lights that prevent the space from seeming a gaping, dark cave. In 1988, Anthony Lumsden of DMJM and Gensler & Associates designed a rooftop reception hall and another underground meeting space that cost $200 million and effectively doubled the size of the facility.

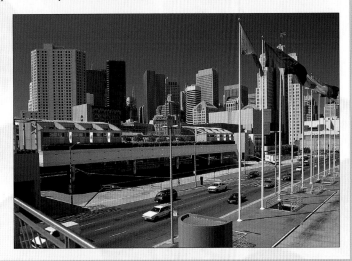

The newest facility, Moscone West, a three story building with a glass façade 350' long and 110' tall, will open in 2003 adding an additional 773,000 square feet of meeting and office space.

SOUTH PARK

Once a place of leisure for the wealthy residents of SOMA in the mid-nineteenth century, South Park declined and then rose again with the fate of the neighborhood. The oval-shaped park was built in 1856 with London's Berkeley Square as a model. At that time it was lined with elegant homes and mansions. A mass exodus of the city's affluent to Nob Hill in the 1870s left the area bereft for over a century. Industry moved into the neighborhood and then moved out, leaving only squalor. Construction of the Bay Bridge in the 1930s did yet more injustice to South Park, and only quite recently did it begin to rebound. The arrival of artists to the area followed by the general development of the neighborhood has brought life back to the park. Once again the park's weeping willows and sycamore trees provide shade for the neighborhood's well-to-do.

SOMA: two view of South Park.

Following pages: a view of SOMA with Pacific Bell Park in the foreground.

Above, the statue of legendary Giants player Willy Mays.

Top, Candlestick Park.

CANDLESTICK AND PACIFIC BELL PARKS

The famous city's field Candlestick Park is home of the five-time Super Bowl champion 49ers. Three miles south of San Francisco via US 101, Candlestick Park seats over 60,000 people. The "Stick," as it is known, was the first stadium to be made entirely of reinforced concrete. Built in 1960 by John S. Bolles and Associates, the stadium sits right on the edge of the Bay, a proximity that makes playing conditions notoriously cool and windy. Pacific Bell Park, home of the San Francisco Giants, opened to rave reviews in April of 2000. The intimate baseball park situated on San Francisco Bay in the South of Market area, seats approximately 41,000 fans. A well struck ball hit to right field can actually clear the stadium and land in the bay waters, now called Mc Covey Cove.

A period photograph of the old San Francisco Airport, point of departure for early transpacific flights, and, below, the San Francisco International Airport, 14 miles (22.5 km) south of the city.

THE AIRPORT

San Francisco boasts a longstanding tradition as regards aviation. In far-off 1925, Pan Am launched the first scheduled service for the Far East, with their China Clipper. Since 1980, the San Francisco International Airport Museum, in collaboration with the San Francisco Museum of Fine Arts, schedules exhibits at the airport terminal on a regular basis. The permanent collection, in the Administration Building, provides the visitor with a fine review of aviation.

San Francisco's
Busy Airport
Mills Field

INDEX